GREENLAND: A VISITORS' PRIMER

A GUIDE TO THE WORLD'S LARGEST ISLAND WHERE THE CLIMATE-CHANGE CLOCK TICKS EVER MORE LOUDLY

by

Michael A. Hutchinson

FRONTICEPIECE

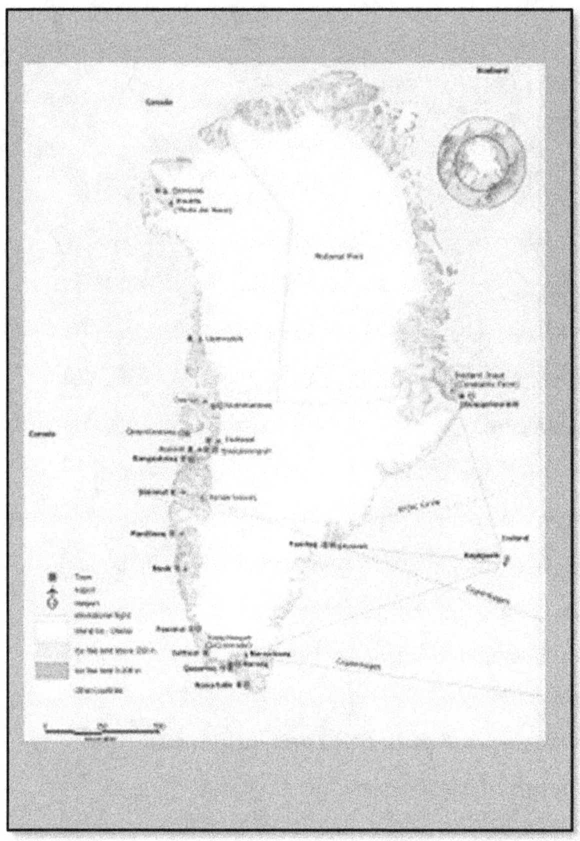

Map of Greenland, showing the main towns and the sea- and air-connections with Iceland and Denmark

CONTENTS

ACKNOWLEDGMENTS

I am fortunate enough to have visited a fair few places, but Greenland has been one of the most memorable. I was enticed there by the idea of 'exploring the unknown' and accepting the challenge of heading somewhere in the colder clime that for me had been 'off the beaten track.' I am grateful to **Lynne** not only for her companionship during this exploration but for her subsequent prompting and encouragement when embarking upon writing this visitors' primer.

I am also indebted to **Lillian and Willie Verhaegen** from Zandhoven in Belgium, without whose kindness I would not have been able to draw upon the wider range of photographic images to illustrate the text. Writing a retrospective guide to a newly-discovered destination can be likened to revisiting that place, this time with a more enquiring eye that takes a wider sweep of the geographical-, historical-, economic- and cultural landscape. A chance reunion with artist Lillian and her husband has allowed me to substitute some of the photographs that had been lost during ongoing image-transfers.

I am indebted to **Brigitte Dahl** from the prize-winning Danish architectural practice **Friis and Moltke**, who most kindly sought out some of the early water-colour paintings of the late **Elmar Moltke**, one of the practice's founding-partners, and granted me permission to include these beautiful pictures in this guide.

Events in Greenland – as in the remainder of the world - are in a constant state of flux, and whilst I have endeavoured to provide the most up to date information, any errors are my sole responsibility, and I shall endeavour to correct them in updated versions of the guide as they come to light.

GREENLAND:
FREQUENTLY ASKED QUESTIONS

SIZE AND POPULATION

With an area of 216.6 million hectares, Greenland is the largest island in the world, with 85% of it covered by ice. This means that only the coastline is inhabited, with a population of 57,000 inhabitants [2011 figures]. The population is dispersed across 18 larger and smaller towns and a series of small settlements. The largest town is the capital **Nuuk**, with almost 16,000 inhabitants. Approximately 15% of the total inhabitants live in small settlements. Around 90% of the population is of **Greenlandic origin**, whereas around 10% [**mostly Danes**] are immigrants.

HOUSEHOLD AND FAMILY PATTERNS IN GREENLAND

The 1993-94 Health Interview Survey in Greenland showed that the average size of households was 3.5, and almost three-fourths of the Greenlandic population lived in families with children. The pattern of these families with children revealed a variety of single-parent families (6% of the total Greenlandic population), nuclear families (42%), extended families (14%), and other types of families (11%).

RELIGION

The prevailing religion in Greenland is [Christian] Protestantism. Greenland is an independent diocese in the Danish Evangelical Lutheran Church with a bishop appointed by Denmark, whose monarch is head of the church. It is the 'official' religion and is followed by about 2/3 of the population, with approximately 1/3 of the population following other forms of Christianity. Traditional beliefs such as Shamanism are followed by a small minority.

EDUCATION AND LITERACY

Greenland's Self Rule Government administers schools. Education is in Greenlandic, with Danish as a foreign language given top priority.

All children in Greenland are entitled to ten years of compulsory education and attend school from the age of six to sixteen. Primary and lower secondary schools comprise three age-bands: the three-year level for the youngest pupils, the four-year level for the middle group and a three-year level for the oldest children.

There 24 town schools and about 60 village schools in Greenland, including 3 high schools, with some 8,500 students in total.

Greenland's sole university, the University of Greenland, (Greenlandic: **Ilisimatusarfik**; Danish: Grønlands **Universitet**) is in Nuuk, and it includes the **Department of Learning (Ilinniarfissuaq)**, the oldest educational facility in Greenland, located in the old colonial part of Nuuk (**Nuutoqaq**: Old Nuuk). The University's Department of Nursing and Health Science, along with the **Nuuk Technical College** and the **Iron & Metal**

School are other notable higher- and further education establishments. The University has a quite small student intake, given, understandably, that most students opt to attend Danish universities, which can offer a wider range of courses.

Literacy in Greenland is recorded as being 99% across all age ranges,[1] but it said that schoolchildren rank very poorly on tests relative to their counterparts in Denmark.

HEALTH AND HEALTH-CARE PROVISION

Health care services are primarily the responsibility of the Government of Greenland. The health care system is obligated to deliver equal health care to all citizens regardless of where they live. All health care services are free, including provision of prescription medicine.

Greenland is divided into 16 health care districts for the purposes of **primary health care**. These districts are based in 16 towns, each with a primary health care clinic [that also doubles as a local hospital] serving that town and a variable number of outlying settlements. The centres in the larger towns have doctors, nurses, health visitors, midwives, medical laboratory technicians, etc. The primary health care clinics in the smaller of the 16 towns have nurses and health care workers. Every person with a permanent address in Greenland has to register with one of the 16 health care districts; and every health care clinic contact made by that person has to be recorded in the countrywide **Electronic Medical Records** system [EMR], which itself is able to identify and

---

[1] The average reading age of the UK population is 9 years, meaning that they have achieved the reading capability normally expected of a 9-year old. The Guardian readership has a reading age of 14 and the Sun newspaper's readership has a reading age of 8.

locate any person so registered. The majority of immigrants (foreign workers) live in Nuuk.

The high level of contact by Greenlanders with the primary health care in Greenland – including that among women - is comparable to other Nordic countries such as Denmark and Iceland. Records for Nuuk show that in general for every age, the most frequent type of contacts relate to **musculoskeletal, respiratory or skin diseases**, except that for children, the most frequent type of contact relates to **ear or respiratory diseases**.

Research has shown that virus/bacteria related conditions such as **Otitis Media, an inflammatory disease of the inner ear**, have grown in significance amongst Greenland's Eskimos – and those of Canada - after the colonization of the island, and most likely to have been caused by the social, cultural, habitary and dietary changes due to the increased contact with the outside world. The aim was therefore to further describe the epidemiological pattern of the different OM disease groups and identify the potentially associated risk factors in Greenlandic children, because these diseases are primarily established and problematical in childhood.

Queen Ingrid's Hospital in its capital, Nuuk, has 156 beds and is both the national hospital for Greenland – being the only one offering a wide range of specialized treatment, in-house and outpatient clinic - and a local hospital for the Nuuk health district.

Greenland has undergone a rapid transition during the last half century from a **traditional Inuit society** dominated by small communities, villages and settlements to a **modern society** with more than 60% of the inhabitants living in towns with at least 2,500 inhabitants. The resultant profound social and cultural changes have resulted in a health transition now reflecting an **increasing prevalence of lifestyle-related diseases such as obesity, diabetes and ischaemic heart disease, a transition similar to that observed among the Inuit peoples in Alaska and**

Canada. Survey results for the period 1995-2010[2] indicated a high prevalence of **DIABETES MELLITUS** [about 1 in 10 adults][3], with between 70% and 80% going undiagnosed. The levels of undiagnosed **HYPERTENSION** were also high, with only a quarter of those with elevated blood pressure treated for hypertension. Awareness of these two chronic lifestyle-related conditions across the population as a whole and in the health care system have been termed `sub-optimal'.

INFANT MORTALITY RATE[4] AND LIFE EXPECTANCY

Total: **8.7** deaths of infants under one year old /1,000 live births (2018 estimate updated 07/12/2019), broken down by gender into male: 9.9 deaths/1,000 live births; female: 7.4 deaths/1,000 live births. By comparison, the equivalent rate in the UK in 2017 increased from **3.9 to 4** deaths per thousand live births. This reflects an increase in neo-natal deaths in the UK from 2.8 to 2.9 for the same year, likely linked with an increase in the number of pre-term births in the UK [after less than 23 weeks' gestation] over the last few years.

Life expectancy in Greenland rose from nearly **64 years in 1979 to nearly 72 in 2013, before tailing off since then. Life**

---

[2] Articles in **International Journal of Circumpolar Health** made public courtesy of **Taylor & Francis**

[3] This might be due to the relatively low level of diagnostic checks undertaken, or patients' reluctance to seek treatment or sub-optimal awareness amongst health care personnel.

[4] **Source:** CIA World Factbook;

expectancy in the UK in 2018 was 79.6 years for males and 83.2 years for females.[5]

ENERGY SOURCES & DISTRIBUTION

Electricity generation[6] is controlled by the state-owned **Nukissiorfiit**. It is distributed at 220 V and 50 Hz and sockets of Danish type K are used. Electricity has historically been generated by oil or diesel power plants, even though there is a large surplus of potential hydropower. Because of rising oil prices, there is a program to build hydro power plants. Since the success of the 1993 Buksefjord dam – whose distribution path to Nuuk includes the Ameralik Span[7] – the long-term policy of the Greenland government is to produce the island's electricity from renewable domestic sources. A third turbine at Buksefjord brought its capacity up to 45 MW in 2008; in 2007, a second, 7.2 MW dam was constructed at Qorlortorsuaq; and in 2010, a third, 15 MW dam was constructed at Sisimiut. In Greenland, the Faroe Islands, Svarlbard and Jan Mayen, the share of renewable energy in the primary energy supply is less than 15%, with Greenland at roughly 15%. The energy supply in Iceland has a significantly different profile. Renewable energy there covers some 87% of the total primary energy supply, primarily in the form of geothermal energy and hydropower.

---

[5] The dramatic UK improvements during the 20th century resulted from universal childhood immunizations, the introduction of universal health care, the treatment of heart disease and cancer, the decline in smoking and life-style changes.

[6] Source: Wikipaedia
[7] The longest spanning overhead electrical power line in the world, 5376 m, near Nuuk

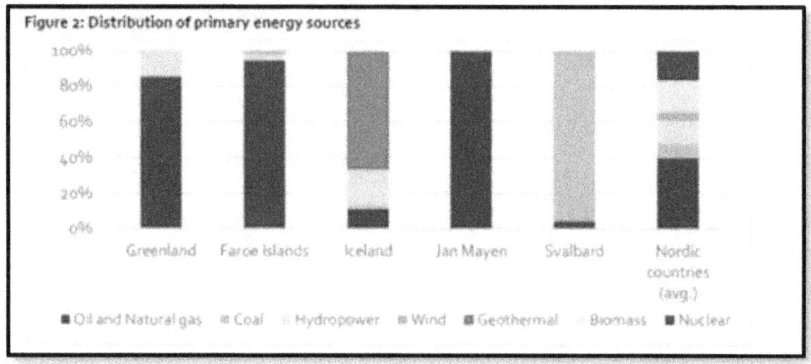

Arctic areas that include Greenland are characterised by long, cold winters and short, cool summers, meaning that heating is required during the whole year. This reduced-fluctuation energy demand for heating provides favourable conditions for optimisation of the available thermal capacities.

The prospect of [inter-]connecting the Arctic islands is a recurring discussion. The benefits are security of supply and economies of scale through being able to supply a larger demand from fewer large generating units. However, the costs of laying power cables at sea over stretches of hundreds of kilometres are considerable.

INTRODUCTION:

MAKING SENSE OF GREENLAND

The aim of this publication is to provide visitors to Greenland with useful and wide-ranging insights into the large, very precious, rapidly changing island and its people. My account has been written from the perspective of an outsider with a background in architecture and landscape architecture who wishes to encourage others to join him in discovering this beautiful but fragile place and its people. The guide inevitably covers aspects of the Greenlanders' economic life that are fluid and sensitive, such as the prospecting of crude oil or the siting of an aluminium smelter, and whilst I have tried to include up-to-date information, I ask the reader to accept that things will change overnight. I hope that the guide will encourage a yearning to understand the dynamics of the island and promote a growing identification with its inhabitants through greater interaction.

It has been said that Greenland's melting has been adopted as the world's problem, not that of the local population of 57,000 people. Voices from the 90% Inuit population have rarely been heard[8]. The Study showed that climate change is having an untold psychological effect on native Greenlanders.

I recall being welcomed by an island community group on a visit to Eastern Canada and enjoying coffee and cake whilst comparing life in Canada and the UK. True, we might need the help of an

---

[8] Source: Greenlandic Perspectives Survey, undertaken by the University of Copenhagen, the Kraks Fond Institute for Urban Economic Research and the University of Greenland; article by Dan McDougall, the *Guardian* newspaper, 12/08/2019

interpreter in Greenland initially, but the benefits would be enormous.

Visitors to Greenland, especially those who step ashore from the tender boats that whisk passengers from the anchored cruise vessels to the small quayside landing-stage, might well ponder on the reaction of the native Inuit populations – especially the children - to the masses of fascinated strangers suddenly thrust in their midst:

"Who on earth are these outsiders and what has brought them here to our little, close-knit community with its unique cultural tradition and its unique geography?"

But of course it is the character of Greenland and the Greenlanders which is Greenland's **Unique Selling Point,** to use marketing terminology. The touristic scene is fast-changing, and Greenland is seeing more and ever-larger cruise-liners docking alongside or anchoring close-by in its deeper harbours. The island's tourism-market is in its infancy, largely because Greenland doesn't as yet have the infrastructure to provide the kind of facilities to which international visitors will be accustomed. Besides which, would it be in the long-term interest of Greenland to encourage a degree of development which could quite easily be self-destructive?[9] The **Galapagos Islands** off the Ecuadorian west coast of South America are home to very rare and precious ecological system that is now recognized internationally as being especially vulnerable to touristic pressure

---

[9] By way of illustration, the economy of the island of Antigua in the Eastern Caribbean is largely dependent upon tourism [70%+ of its Gross Domestic Product [GDP]] and the impact of visitor-facilities on the places of interest can be overwhelming.

and development of any sort. Greenland's position is different but no less valuable for that.

Clearly, a balance needs to be struck between Greenland and the Greenlanders on the one hand and the demands of tourists on the other. But who is in a position to decide how far the islanders wish to embrace tourism, and what time /resources do they can expend on it?

 Whether walking through a town or village or heading over rough terrain towards a glacier, visitors want to make sense of what they see and have a fuller appreciation of the dynamics underpinning the every-day life of Greenlanders, literally as much as metaphorically. Enjoy your visit, because if you blink twice, the Greenland of yesterday may be gone!

Travelling to Greenland is less straightforward than going to many of the normal holiday destinations because its main settlements are few in number, relatively small and not particularly accessible.   Access to them by sea is largely dependent upon harbours being ice-free, meaning arriving and leaving in the short late-spring-to early-autumn window. Air travel is slightly different insofar as runways can be kept relatively ice-free for a longer period of time. Yet today the number of airports/ airfields in Greenland can be counted on one hand. And once the visitors have landed, they have to be able to move on to their destination in Greenland …. generally without the benefit of interconnecting roads. And, if coastal sea-travel is ruled out by ice-bound harbours, then short journeys can be made by snowmobiles or dog-drawn sleds across frozen sea-ice or by light-aircraft/helicopter or by 'accessible' tracks, often using off-the-road vehicles. However, with the prolonged melting of sea-ice, travelling across this is becoming increasingly hazardous and frustrating for the local populace.

For wheelchair-using cruise-visitors, the transfer from ship to shore can be problematic, notably when the ship has to anchor offshore, tenders are employed to transfer people ashore and the water is choppy. If visitors can use walkers and sloping gangways from variable cruise-liner disembarkation decks can replace steps, this will make it easier for them, especially if they are accompanied. However, for all visitors, these challenges form part of their Greenland adventure, and I hope that they find my short guide helpful.

ooooooooooOOOOOOOOOOOOooooooooooooo

Greenland and its melting ice-cap may have hit the political headlines recently, especially in the West, doubtless because some – **but not all** – 'developed'-nations have calculated that they might be seen in a better Public Relations light if signing up for carbon-reduction / carbon-neutral targets.[10] Yet, whilst the likes of the UK might aim to switch from – for example – coal- and gas-fired electricity power stations to wind-farms, biomass, hydro-electricity and the increased use of nuclear power, the likes of China and the USA are reluctant to stop using coal for power generation, although it is obviously counter-productive in the global sense. During the post-WW2 era of German division, Eastern Germany [the DDR] relied extensively on its brown peat in order to fuel its electricity power stations, delivering a double

---

[10] And there was the occasion in 2019 when US President Trump announced that his country was considering purchasing Greenland from Denmark

environmental whammy. In that sense the World Community, some 7+ decades on, is still dragging its feet.[11]

Measures to reduce the UK'S reliance upon petrol/diesel cars and goods vehicles by providing significant inducements to switch to more environmentally-friendly transport, will have longer-term benefits if production can be scaled-up to make them affordable for the mass market. Only then might we could significantly reduce carbon – and other toxic – emissions and take a huge step forward in advancing our Green credentials and **help Greenland in the process!** However, these steps have to be part of a real global effort, with governments - individually and collectively - willing to stand firm against powerful corporations and vested interests for the sake of future generations.

But time is not on the side of Greenland or anywhere else in our self-destructive world. The island and its people have arrived at a critical juncture. Right now, Greenland is in a state of flux, and both the island and its indigenous population are extremely vulnerable in the face of the impact of a mix of enormous pressures bearing down from all directions:

- **a rapidly evolving and diversifying domestic economy;**
- **accelerating global warming, with its profound knock-on effects;**
- **a sudden break with traditional culture/living;**

---

[11] The UK's Times newspaper of 24.01.2020 reported Prime Minister Johnson's agreement to terminate the UK's financial support for fossil-fuel electricity generation projects in certain under-developed countries as part of its effort to counter global warming.

- **the increasing interest of exploitative mineral prospectors worldwide in the resources of Greenland;**
- **handling the struggle for economic survival whilst striving for complete autonomy from Denmark;**
- **dealing quickly and safely with the toxic waste left behind by the United States at Camp Century and Project Ice Worm.[12]**

Financial wealth and serious poverty run in parallel amongst the island's populace, with a widening gap between them. Whilst this is a particularly significant factor that both Greenland and Denmark wish to address, the question is: how?   Can Greenlanders collectively harness their energy and knowledge to bring about long-term solutions that are in the interest of all the islanders?[13] Time may not be on their side, nor indeed for the populace of the whole world!

------

[12] The abandoned sunken nuclear-powered base constructed at the outset of the Cold War in the early 1950s is becoming increasingly exposed to the atmosphere due to the melting of the icecap, and the nuclear waste and asbestos need to be dealt with safely. In fact, there are about 30 abandoned sites dating back to that era.

[13] 09/08/2019: A UK Channel 4 News journalist reports tonight on his visit to the west coast of Greenland, north of the Arctic Circle. He notes the alarming acceleration of ice melt from the island's snow cap and its ramifications, especially its contribution to the huge rise in global sea level on the drowning of land and settlements across all continents: low-lying Europe, the Indian sub-continent, the Far-East. He then sets this in the context of commercial voices on Greenland who welcome the freeing up of seaway routes to increased trade with China. I discuss uranium prospecting for the Chinese market later in this booklet. Channel 4 News has been labelled by those it challenges as `The Harbinger of Doom'; but the realists amongst us like to see `un-redacted truth' for what it is, if that is discernible!

Yet, paradoxically, Greenland might be in an advantageous position.[14] Terrain and climate have thus far been major factors in the absence of a road-infrastructure. However, climate change will bring about opportunities for a creative and sympathetic response to ongoing connectivity between the island's communities.

---

[14] Inhabitants of a small villages like **Boca da Valeria**, lying on the southern bank of the **Amazon River in Parintins Province in Brazil**, do not have most of the goods or facilities deemed to be essential in Western societies: mains electricity and drainage, infant-, junior- and secondary schools, homes with electrical gadgets and equipment, etc., etc. Yet the community is a happy and healthy and self-supporting family, and without the crime endemic of so many cities in Western culture. Their canoes and small fishing boats might have outboard petrol engines, but these are small concessions to the way of life of 'developed' countries.

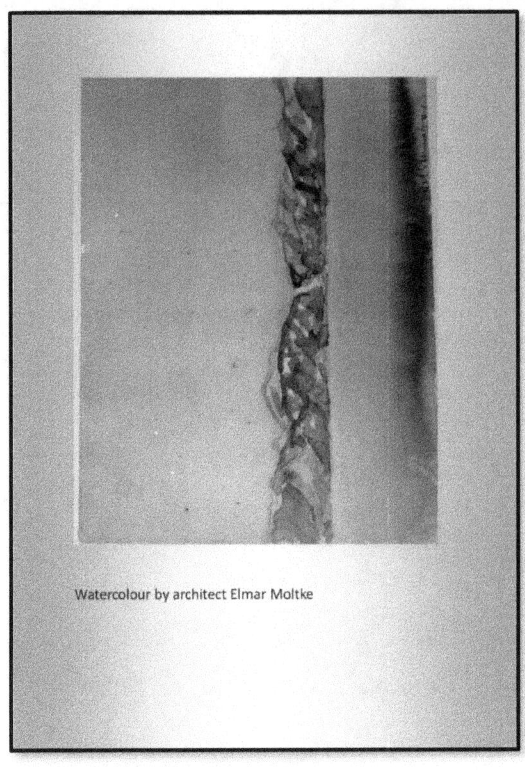

Watercolour by architect Elmar Moltke

CHAPTER ONE:

GREENLAND'S PHYSICAL GEOGRAPHY + ECONOMIC GEOLOGY

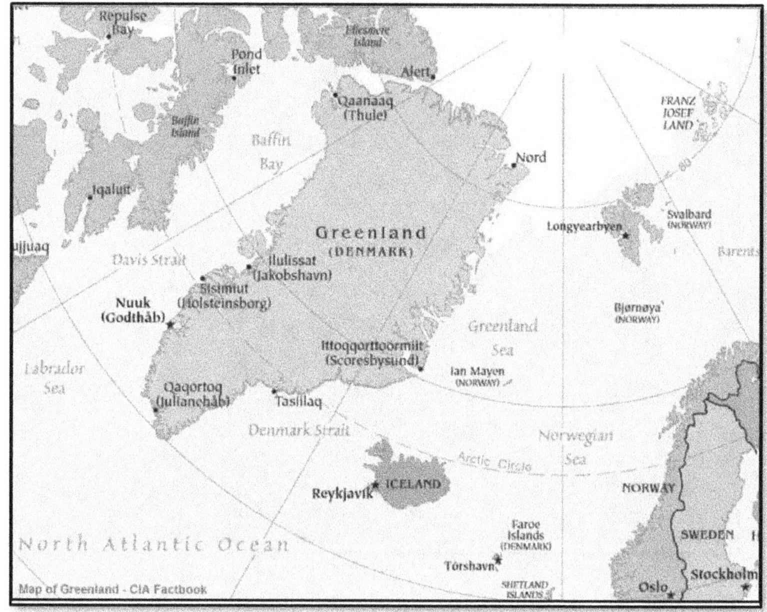

Map of Greenland, showing its relationship to Canada and Scandinavia respectively; map courtesy CIA Facebook

Greenland

Towns in Greenland

Society and life in Greenland offer a complete contrast to those of Western Europe in so many ways. Greenland has never known the Industrial Revolution in the form familiar to us in the UK, nor the size, density and nature of the population concentrations in settlements that grew as a concomitant of the outworking of that Revolution.

More recently, Greenland has held a unique strategic politico-geographic position since the outplaying of World War Two and the Cold War from the 1950s to the late 1980s. And even though the original US airbase at **Kangerlussuaq** has long since closed[15], the US retains this unique rôle on this large island on the Arctic Circle, a former dependency that is part of the larger Danish sovereignty that includes **the Faroe Islands and mainland Denmark.** The US Government initially took an interest in Greenland during World War Two, when Denmark was occupied by Germany. Greenland's strategic location, sitting between the United States and war-torn Europe, meant that it was crucial for the Allies that Greenland did not fall into enemy hands. Greenland was a major stopover for Allied aircraft heading across the Atlantic, and weather stations around Greenland provided data for the development of accurate European weather reports that were crucial to the Allied forces' success.

"The Allies had to occupy Greenland because they did not want Germany to do so first," says author **Kristine Harper**. On the same day in 1941 that German troops marched across the border into Denmark, the United States agreed to deliver goods to, and take over the defence of Greenland. Denmark allowed the Americans to build military bases in return for recognition of Danish sovereignty. The Americans immediately built runways and military bases and installed research stations. They trained about 7,000 meteorologists and sent some of them to weather stations located in the Arctic. In 1944, the American contingency in Greenland consisted of 5,795 military personnel and civilians,

---

[15] Being succeeded by a smallish civilian airport acting as the reception-point for inward-bound freight for Greenland as well as for passenger-air transport

which was just under 25 percent of the entire population. By the end of the war, the US Army Weather Service had installed 14 weather stations while serving 13 Danish-owned stations listed before the war. They had even claimed several secret German weather stations located on Greenland's easily accessible east coast.

ooooooOOOOOOOoooooooo

Greenland today is being tugged in all directions by a combination of forces, notably:

[a]   its striving for full and complete economic- and political independence;

[b]   the tensions between the Greenlandic Administration and oil- and mineral prospectors on the one hand, and the likes of Greenpeace and other smaller and larger environmental-protection activists on the other who seek to prevent Greenland's unique character and geographical/ecological character from being irrevocably damaged;

[c]   the knock-on effects of Greenland's strategic position in relation to military jostling between the world's super-powers;

At this point in time – two decades into the 21st century and in a period witnessing a quickening rate of physical change - the island of Greenland comprises a huge ice-cap with a few settlements squeezed in along its habitable eastern- and western margins, confined to the narrow sides and heads of its numerous small, long and large fjords. But change is already underway.

GREENLAND'S PRINCIPAL GEOLOGICAL/CLIMATIC/LANDSCAPE ZONES

Greenland is the world's largest island, though four-fifths of the land area lies beneath the second largest ice cap in the world. The

island can be divided into landscape-zones that reflect their geological nature and their positioning in relation to the Arctic Circle and North Pole. Ice-free areas are presently restricted to the coastal fringes, divisible into two **biogeographic regions: the Low- and the High Arctic Tundra**.

The **High Arctic** region is located above 75° N latitude at **Melville Bay** on the West Coast and 70° N at **Scoresby Sound**, on the East Coast. In a few areas, the ice sheet extends all the way to the coast; the ice-free land of the north is concentrated along the northeast coast. This region is less mountainous than the southern portion, with some rolling hills, such as in **Peary Land** at the extreme northeast. At 80° N latitude, Peary Land is the most northern ice-free landmass in the world. Younger in origin than southern Greenland, the land is mostly composed of **Paleozoic Age gneiss**[16] and **sedimentary rock**. Clues as to the origin of its rocks lie in the combination of glistening speckles of broken boulders and the folding of initial sedimentary layers. Metamorphosis - a combination of extreme pressure and heat – has fundamentally transformed the nature of the sedimentary

---

[16] This western **gneiss** complex is approximately 3600 million years old. The Isua Greenstone Belt in southwest **Greenland**, is extraordinary in that it contains some of the oldest bedrock on the planet, approximately 3800 million years old. Gneiss is a metamorphic rock with a banded or foliated structure, often coarse-grained and comprised mainly of feldspar, quartz and mica.

material. A combination of these altered rocks, ocean-floor volcanic intrusions and Earth's-mantle rocks has given us an exciting skyline of prolific jagged, spiked pikes and snow-filled glacial cwms, more often than not harbouring snow- and ice-pockets to remind us that even at the height of its shortened summer the chill, barren landscape rules supreme at high altitudes. Unlike neighbouring **Iceland**, there are no geysers releasing the jets of boiling water and sulphur gas into the atmosphere. Greenland instead reveals its periphery of rocks that are hard, granite-like in nature, periodically displaying colour-banding indicative of their origin as among the oldest on earth.

Post-glacial landscape images, with remnants of cwms, hanging-valleys, glacial moraine and glacial melt

Miniature fresh-water lakes abound, where the melting ice has left hollows in its wake, filled with fresh-water often - though not necessarily - linked to river-systems. Streams rush down toward valley-floors, sometimes thundering over spectacular hanging-valley waterfalls on their way down.

The geological map included above looks complex and intimidating to those of us not versed in geological terminology. In simpler terms, we see the evidence of folding, buckling and

Greenland's geological map: the Rae craton to the north and the North Atlantic craton to the south dominate the island, emerging from under the icecap in narrow zones at the coast; source: Wikipaedia

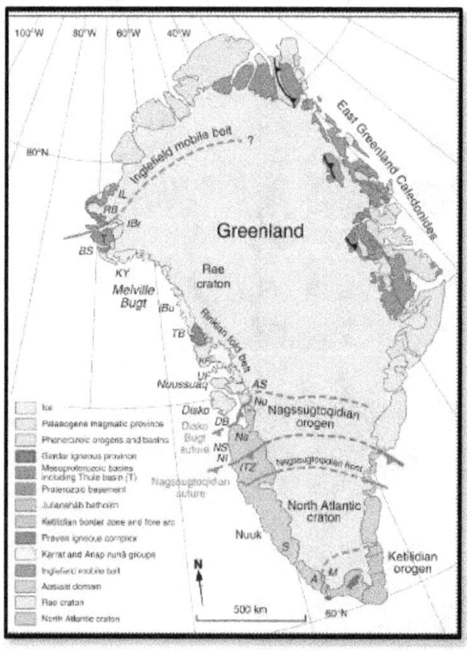

sliding of elements of the earth's crust, giving rise to ridges, troughs and the mountainous elements of the country's exciting landscape, along with the exposure of igneous basalt[17] intrusions along the periphery of the island. The climate of northern Greenland is **arctic**, and the lower soil layer is permanently frozen and called **permafrost**. Summer temperatures generally do not exceed 5°C in the High Arctic region, and the north has a higher pressure system than the south, resulting in less precipitation. Rainfall decreases inland, and thus, arctic "desert" occurs near the ice cap in many places.

Greenland experiences a few unusual meteorological phenomena, such the sudden and sometimes **violent catabatic and Föhn winds. Föhn winds** are warm, dry air masses that blow from the ice cap to the coast and that are able to raise temperatures by 10-20°C, thereby removing and melting snow.

VEGETATION

The typical North Greenlandic vegetation type is the **Arctic Tundra**, a kind of semi-desert in which any vegetation capable of surviving the severe climate and terrain is sparse, low-growing and not particularly species-rich. **The short growing-season, the climatic harshness and the lack of topsoil of any significant depth mean that plant-growth is seriously stunted.** The coastal high arctic plant belt does not have willow scrub or herb slopes as in the south, but is instead covered with **heath, fellfield, and snow patches**. Plants are very specifically adapted to the extreme climate of this region, being able to tolerate dark winters, arctic

---

[17] **Basalt** is a dark-coloured, fine-grained, **igneous** rock composed mainly of plagioclase and pyroxene minerals. It most commonly forms as an extrusive rock, such as a lava flow, but can also form in small intrusive bodies, such as an **igneous** dike or a thin sill. It has a composition similar to gabbro.

temperatures, and low precipitation that primarily falls as snow. Species include **striking varieties of wildflowers such as sulphur-colored buttercup, alpine foxtail, and nodding lychnis**. These examples are so well adapted that they cannot exist at warmer temperatures, and are generally **absent from the Low Arctic Tundra**. The present vegetation of the **High Arctic Tundra** is sparse and not highly developed due to the brief and cold growing season. The present vegetation of the **High Arctic Tundra** is sparse and not highly developed due to the brief and cold growing season. Communities are concentrated on the east coast of Greenland, gradually becoming sparser from south to north. Certain species or communities occur to the north only in association with hot springs, which are particularly numerous in **the basalt areas** on the central eastern coast. Examples of these species are **Epilobium palustre** and **Platanthera hyperborea**.

MAMMALS

There are three latitudinal regions along the east coast: **Jameson Land** at the transition from low arctic to high arctic, **the mid-coast from 72° – 79° N**, and **Peary Land** at the northernmost extreme of Greenland as well as the world.

Nine species of terrestrial mammals are native to Greenland: arctic hare, arctic fox – (white and blue subspecies), arctic wolf, caribou or reindeer, polar bear, muskox, ermine, arctic hare, collared lemming, and the wolverine. Aside from the polar bear - which is a partially marine creature and has little trouble migrating - Greenland's larger mammals, including humans, reached the island from the northwest over winter ice. Several of these mammals could not cross the large glaciers of Melville Bay in the west, or the Blosseville Kyst on the East Coast, being found solely in the **northern high arctic tundra** region.

Almost all of **Northeastern Greenland** falls within **the largest national park in the world.** This region is a major breeding area for the **muskox** and the threatened **polar bear**. Marine mammals in the vicinity include **Atlantic walrus, bearded seal, harp seal, ringed seal along all the coasts, and hooded seal in the southern fjords.** Greenland's **high arctic** serves as a breeding ground for many bird species during summer. These **include Great northern diver, Barnacle goose, Pink-footed goose, Common eider, King eider, Gyrfalcon, Snowy owl, Sanderling, Knot, Ptarmigan and Raven.**

In the coastal periphery of **lower Arctic Greenland**, beyond the mountainous interior, shrubby-species include birch and willow, but even these stunted plants only attain a height of two or so metres at best, with the willow generally less than a metre in height.

Rough, thin and patchy grassland partially cover the hillsides. Herbaceous plants other than the coarser grasses are rare treasures in this part of Greenland, and include **cotton grasses –** often found in poorly-drained bogs - and several particularly colourful plants popping up as gems in the relative sparsity of its vegetative landscape. This provides notional grazing for the reindeer and foxes, which enrich their diet with their cull of small vertebrates when opportunity permits. Herbaceous plants other than the coarser grasses are rare treasures in this part of Greenland, and include **cotton grasses –** often found in poorly-drained bogs - and several particularly colourful plants popping up as gems in the relative sparsity of its vegetative landscape.

A snapshot of plants and animals adapted to the difficult climate and terrain of Greenland

CHAPTER TWO

EARLY HUMAN HABITATION TO 19TH CENTURY COLONIALISM

PRE-HISTORY TO 17TH CENTURY

Human habitation of Greenland dates back perhaps four thousand years, when people from the Siberian Arctic,

Map source: The Encyclopedia Of The Earth: Oceans and Islands

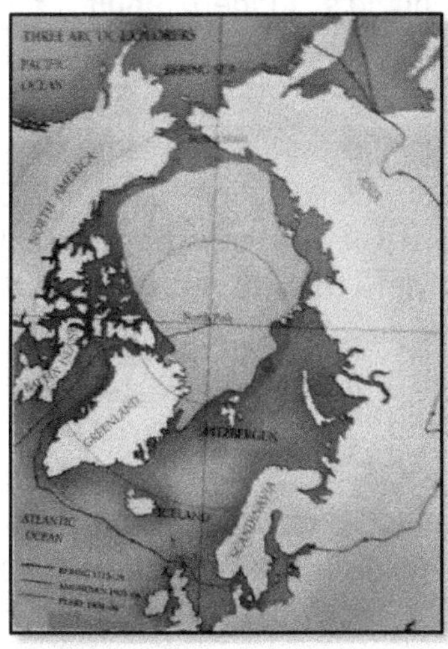

Newfoundland and other parts of what is now the Polar region made their way eastwards across the Baring Sea, Greenlandic Sea and northern Arctic Ocean. Later visitors and settlers - including the Vikings travelled westwards past Iceland from Norway, Sweden and Denmark.

Early settlement in **Sisimiut** probably began over 4,500 years ago with the arrival of the **Saqqaq** people from **Ellesmere Island** in Canada. DNA analysis suggests that the Saqqaqs migrated circumpolar fashion to Arctic Canada and Greenland from **Siberia** about 4,500 years ago, and lived in chilly isolation for more than three millennia. These were followed two or more millennia later by the eskimo **Dorset People** and their stone-age nomadic hunting culture which lasted from about 600 BC to around 200 AD. These **Dorset people** from Canada are known only by what they left behind, including primitive stone tools and beautiful wooden and ivory figurines. They in turn were followed a thousand years ago by the **Thule culture**, again from **Canada.** In the tenth century, the Thule Culture spread across Greenland. This culture, which developed early kayaks, harpoons, and dogsleds, either absorbed or supplanted existing eskimo cultures. Anthropologists agree that Greenland's modern Inuits are descended from the Thule Peoples.

Thule influence spread across the island during the same time that Norse explorers first investigated its coastlines. About 900 AD, a Norwegian named **Gunnbjørn Ulfsson** became the first European to set foot on Greenland. More than 80 years later, **Erik the Red**, followed. He organized the first Viking settlements on the island. Around 1000, Leif Eriksson, son of Erik the Red, brought Christianity to Greenland from Norway. Norse settlements prospered for about 500 years, thanks in large measure to continuing ties with Iceland and Norway, but these settlements eventually dissolved and disappeared. Whilst their disappearance has been attributed to climatic changes and problems with the Thule tribes, their demise remains largely shrouded in mystery.

Human habitation in the form of subsistence survival has always been limited to small areas along the coast or fjords, and whilst there are a number of small settlements in north-western Greenland, the northern limit for modest communities is not much farther north than **Tasiilaq** in Eastern Greenland and a bit further north of **Sisimiut** on the west coast.

The early inhabitants were relatively accustomed to the nature of Greenland's climate and terrain: the long winters with scarcely an hour or two of daylight merging into a very short summer period and virtually perpetual daylight. These folk co-existed with polar bears, reindeer, the Arctic fox and other mammals perfectly adapted to their harsh habitat, so that whilst these animals were hunted for their flesh, fur and skins, the **Inuits'** diet in summer was centred on fish. The main form of transport around the inhabited part of the coast was by way of the boat, canoe or kayak, and when the sea and the fjords were frozen over in winter, the inhabitants relied upon the wooden sleds drawn by husky dogs.

Given the inhospitable nature of the place, it is not surprising that many folk were nomadic, moving around to suit the time of year, the weather and the opportunities for finding food. Hunting of **muskoxen** along with the culling of **whales** and **seals**, provided the principle source of food for many of Greenland's people, but the much more recent use of dogs to force the muskcox herd to form a defensive circle made them particularly prone to the hunters' rifles as a larger scale method of culling.

17TH CENTURY ONWARDS

Many mammals were hunted close to extinction by Greenlanders in the 19th- and earlier 20th centuries, even though the country's human population only numbered about 56,000 in the year 2000.

European whalers arrived in Sisimiut in the 17th century, and with the arrival of **the missionary Hans Egeda** in 1721 and the subsequent establishment of relations between the native Inuits and the Europeans, regular contact between these two peoples was established. Sisimiut's first houses followed colonization by the missionary and date back to 1756, with the blue church inaugurated in 1775. **Hans Egede** came to Greenland to find the Catholic Norwegians so that he could convert them into the 'proper' (Reformed) Christian doctrine.

Egede and his successors (1721-1832), hoped that they could find descendants of the Norwegians whom they knew had lived in Greenland since 982. The connection between Greenland and the other Nordic countries was lost just before the year 1500, when there were still Norwegians in the country. From 1829 to 1831, Captain Graah's expedition reached so far up the east coast that he could conclude that the Norse people were no longer present in Greenland. In 1953 a new Danish constitution made Greenland a part of Denmark, and financial aid to the island increased dramatically. In 1979, a popular referendum gave Greenland "Home Rule" status as a distinct nation within the Kingdom of Denmark.

For centuries, the normal dwelling in Greenland was a **skin tent** during summer and a **peat house** during winter. The peat houses were in principle "throwaway houses", since they would normally only be used for one winter due to the nomadic lifestyle of the Inuit.

This pattern changed quite quickly after the first permanent colonial settlement in the 18th century. Drawings from the early 19th century indicate that the traditional one-winter-only peat houses had evolved into more permanent dwellings, always in close proximity to the colonies of the missionaries and the [Danish] trading company.

Here was Greenland, a collection of relatively self-sufficient coastal communities whose lives, for so long, were determined largely by the geography of the island and the intentions of the Danish-Norwegian traders who, along with the missionaries, colonised the island in eighteenth century. This colonial period lasted from the mid-18th century to 1953, when the island's status as a subordinated dependency officially ended. Its integration with the Danish kingdom now meant that it was on par with other [Danish] municipalities when it came to deciding on the future of natural resources industries on the Arctic's largest island.

GREENLAND AND COPENAGEN: 'COLONY AND METROPOLIS'

Such is the attention paid to them by anthropologists, sociologists, social-historians, etc. that Greenlanders must sometimes feel as if they live in a goldfish bowl! For example, historian Søren Rud once remarked

*"..... I have looked at what the colony and the metropolis had in common: specifically, how the Danish bourgeoisie generally behaved and acted towards the people they regarded as their opposites on the social scale, namely the poorest workers in Copenhagen and the indigenous people of Greenland. They did however try to raise the standard of living of the lower classes through various initiatives. And in both places **the aim was to instil bourgeois values such as cleanliness, diligence and skill** and to direct them to **take themselves out of poverty,"** This was basically the starting point for **Søren Rudd's** recent doctoral thesis: **'Subjugation processes in metropolis and colony: Copenhagen and Greenland in the 19th century '**. Through her

work, the historian offers a new perspective on how Danish-Greenlandic colonial history.

"Opposite to the [lives of Danish] Kingdom's best citizens, they [the Greenlanders] lived miserable and impoverished lives. They stank and were undisciplined and lazy. And because they were unable to drag themselves out of their hopeless life-situation, they had to be helped on their way to a higher standard of living…."

In the past, Earlier history writing had focused on particularly important people in the administration, was replaced n the 1960s by a more indignant narrative was initiated showing the influence of the Danish colonial power in Greenland and focussing on Greenland as a closed space.

In **Copenhagen**, the bourgeoisie started by establishing charitable associations, which was completely in line with the current liberal way of dealing with poverty.

By way of contrast, in the **colony of Greenland** it was primarily the missionaries, doctors, inspectors and colonial administrators who - through the establishment of various citizenship initiatives - propelled the Greenlanders towards diligence and endeavour.

That said, differentiation between the **'haves'** and the **'have nots'** in Greenland's relationship with Denmark is nothing new. The Netherlands and some of its `colonial dependencies' are said to have experienced similar divisions of wealth.

Greenland's first newspaper, the **Atuaqaqdliutt**, founded in **Nuuk** in **1861**, believed that the Greenlanders had lost too much of their identity due to Danish influence. The commentator **Rud** believes that in Greenland, the aim of colonial leadership was all about keeping the Greenlanders *'in the [fish] catch and traditional way of life - in the literal sense'*, not disturbing the status quo .... So being **'Danish'**, but not too Danish, seemed to be the order of the day. ..... Besides which, it would be economically detrimental to the **Royal Greenland Trading Company** [KGH/RGTD] if Greenlanders were no longer able to catch seals and live in the traditional way..... Suffice to say that

Statute of missionary Hans Egeda in Nuuk

the sentiment continues to resonate across the world!

The nett effect for Greenlanders was that they found it more difficult to step out of their 'Greenland' than for the poor Copenhagener to climb the social ladder in the big Danish city. The emergence of the ethnic-tag **'Greenlandic Origin'** did not help social mobility either.

Additionally – in more recent times - **Greenpeace's anti- whaling and anti- sealing campaign in the last decades of the 20th century** is said to have destroyed Greenland's economic base, especially in northern Greenland, where the subsistence-hunting had hitherto made up about 80% of the hunters' income.

However, regulated hunting is permitted today, including inside the huge National Park of North- and East Greenland.

Climatic change, as already noted, forms another threat to the existence of these sea creatures, and when the **caribou** migrated westwards from the National Park around 1900 in search of food, the **arctic wolf** lost it main source of food and did not survive as a species beyond 1934. Some hunters would construct so-called peat houses, which were essentially sheltered recesses on the hillside, extended outwards by the use of boulders covered by moss-peat sods. Some of these have been traced and mapped to form an important record of Greenland's social heritage.

KGH/RGTD held a monopoly on trade from the 1700s until 1950, when the **G-50 law** made it possible for small local craft companies, kiosks - and later the cooperative factory Sipineq in **Sisimiut** - to begin trading on their own account. This new legislation also spurred the (Danish) state to become interested in investing in the town. These imperial trappings were replaced by modern 'merchant adventurers/investors'.

Trade, shipping and transport have had a tremendous effect on the development of the town, not only in the past, but also in recent years. Sisimiut's location and natural features work in its favour, with the harbour-area being big enough to receive both containerships and cargo from the biggest airport in the country: Kangerlussuaq.

TERRA NULLIUS AND SOVEREIGNTY

Arctic exploration has cast doubt over claims of Danish sovereignty over the whole of Greenland: the principle of *terra* *nullius* seemed to leave huge tracts of the territory available to new entrants. Denmark responded by slowly acquiring diplomatic agreements recognizing its sovereignty from the parties involved, beginning with the treaty selling the Danish Virgin Islands to the United States in 1917. Norway – which had become independent of Sweden in 1905 – eventually protested and claimed **Erik the Red's Land** in eastern Greenland during 1931. The Permanent Court of International Justice ruled against Norway two years later, albeit on questionable grounds.

The fall of Denmark to the Nazis in early 1940 increased the power and importance of Greenland's governors greatly, but by 1941 the island had become an American protectorate. Following the war, the former corporate policy was discontinued: the North and South Greenland colonies were united and the RGTD's monopoly officially ended in 1953. Greenland's colonial status was avowedly ended when it was made an integral part of the Kingdom of Denmark[18] with representation in the Danish Parliament, the **Folketing**. In 1979, the **Folketing granted the island home rule** and, in 2009, all matters other than defense and foreign policy were transferred to the regional parliament in Nuuk.

Collecting ice for drinking water in Qaanaaq. In Greenland's subarctic climate, temperatures average only 10 degrees C. at the height of summer, and only along the southwest coast.

---

[18] I guess on the lines of Martinique and other French overseas Départments

CHAPTER THREE:

GREENLANDERS' PATH TO HEARTH AND HOME

Greenland's hamlets, villages and small towns are relatively recent phenomena going back perhaps a century or two, and certainly nothing like the eight or more centuries of a number of England's settlements. And whilst timber from the many forests in the UK offered a plentiful supply of wood, the opposite was the case in Greenland, where timber – as a very precious commodity - would likely have to be brought in by boat in summer. Timber-board cottages were typical of the more permanent Greenlandic homes, with the tradition continuing to the present day in many places.

For centuries, the normal dwelling in Greenland was a **skin tent** during summer and a **peat house** during winter. The peat houses were in principle "throwaway houses", as they would normally only be used for one winter due to the nomadic lifestyle of the Inuit.

This pattern changed quite quickly after the **first permanent colonial settlement in the 18th century.** Drawings from the early 19th century indicate that the traditional one-winter-only peat houses had been turned into more permanent dwellings, always in close proximity to the colonies of the missionaries and the trading company.

Throughout the 19th century and during the first half of the 20th century the traditional peat houses were gradually transformed into small wooden houses. A standard house for the Inuit family at the beginning of the 20th century was a single-roomed, single-storey house with a layer of wooden boards, which acted as walls

Wigwam-type skin tent home in Greenland, useful for nomadic hunting existence; source: Wikipaedia

and an inclined roof, which created room for storage. For insulation, these houses had a thick outer wall made in the traditional way with layers of peat and flat stones.

Until the start of Greenland's intensive modernisation period in the 1950s, Inuit housing was almost exclusively a 'do-it-yourself' initiative, but this was soon to change dramatically. The age of modernisation emerged after 1950 with the Danish Government's formation of the public authority Grønlands Tekniske Organisation (GTO). At that time Greenland was still almost 100% administrated from Copenhagen. The GTO was in charge of orchestrating the transformation of Greenland's infrastructure from that of an archaic, colonial museum into a modern, streamlined society. Very important here was the decision to create up-to-date housing. This was to be developed in two stages. For the approximately 75 smaller settlements, the GTO constructed a set of new houses with proper insulation, wooden floors and windows.

The social history of any country is the charting of the growing aspirations of its people, and Greenland is no exception. Most times, these aspirations will ultimately be translated into physical development. This in turn will determine both individual- and overall prosperity, with both inevitably impacting upon the underlying natural beauty of this island and its people.

The majority of **Greenland's** population now lives in towns. There are about 48,000 inhabitants in the 16 towns of **Greenland** and the other 8,500 people **live** in the country's 60 settlements. For most of the 19 towns, the strategy used was somewhat different. A **town** was defined as the major settlement/inhabited area in each municipality. All other inhabited places within the municipalities were simply classed as **settlements.** The number of municipalities changed little in these years.

Since the establishment of the Greenland Technical Organisation (GTO) in 1950, Greenland has been moving inexorably towards the creation of a 'modern'/urban society. This process has however been more visible in some periods than in others.

Whilst this was a huge step forward, the people for whom these houses were intended were, however, unable to provide any financing of their own. Therefore, loans, which did not need to be repaid for thirty years were introduced. Yet, in retrospect, although the system had seemed to work well for decades, it was ultimately concluded that those who were unable to pay the loan at the outset were unlikely to be able to pay it thirty years later. Subsequently most of these loans were simply written off.

Low-, medium- and high-rise houses and apartments to be seen in Nuuk and the smaller coastal towns in Greenland today

In the towns, blocks of flats with running water and modern toilets were built during the 1950s and the 1960s. As a result, the majority of the inhabitants in the towns became tenants in state-owned modern housing developments. Rents were kept artificially low, as a majority of tenants would simply not be able to pay a market rent.

It was characteristic of the attitude of ruling European governments and their civil servants of the period that a good number decided that their response to the need for mass-housing was the construction of **huge, inhumanely scaled, reinforced-concrete blocks of flats.**

In Britain, a similar type of development was undertaken on an enormous scale across the country.[19] In Greenland, the Danish Government built the huge Block P, the largest building not only in Greenland but in Denmark as a whole.

Even in Greenland, public-housing problems seem to be typical: waiting lists run into decades, structural design remains monotonous and anti-urban, and maintenance woes persist. Consequently, most migrants seek out employer-owned housing. Indeed, similar woes with the American experience—though less constrained by extreme weather or isolation—have given rise to a new consensus around housing vouchers, which permit working families to decide where and how they live. Greenland's experience with housing reminds us that it's equally unrealistic to

---

[19] The social housing at the Elephant and Castle on the south side of the River Thames in London designed by the architect Erno Goldfinger, is normally accepted as a notable representation of this Brutalist social architecture in the UK

believe that state bureaucrats can sympathetically plan where and how people live.

A town was defined officially as the major inhabited area in each municipality. All other inhabited places within the municipalities were defined as settlements. The number of municipalities changed little in the mids. -20th century. In the towns, blocks of flats with running water and modern toilets were built during the 1950s and the 1960s, as a consequence of which the majority of the inhabitants in the towns became tenants in state-owned modern housing developments. Rents were kept artificially low, since the majority of tenants would simply not have been able to pay market rent.

During this period and through the 1980s, a small group, mostly Danes and members of some of Greenland's upper-class clan families, emerged, gaining huge wealth. Some of this wealth was put into large, private houses of some 200 square metres floor-area, which constitutes a luxury house in Greenland. In all of Greenland's towns, specific areas are characterized by being dominated by a small number of such houses in the smaller towns and up to fifty plus in Nuuk. Ever since the 1950s there has been - and indeed there remains - a small and highly lucrative market for these houses. Supply and demand for these luxury houses has roughly been in balance since the early 2000s.

People living in these houses include successful entrepreneurs, shrimp trawler owners, directors in the state owned organisations, top civil servants, and politicians. Thus, their wealth comes from very different sources, and this group of citizens with high incomes shares little except their taste for more luxurious surroundings in their everyday lives. **At the end of the 1980s, a new economic reality began to emerge. Previously the**

state had owned almost 90% of all houses on the transferable housing market aimed at the middle-income groups. The system was however proving to be simply too expensive to maintain and had to be changed.

We have seen that under Danish colonialism, Greenland[20] came to be regarded as peripheral, but since the 1950s, Danes and Greenlanders have sought to transform Greenland into its own place. **Nuuk** grew into a city and a political, administrative and economic centre relative to Greenland's small settlements, which came to be seen as central to Greenlandic culture. Nuuk's rapid growth – dependent on imported Danish designs, materials, technologies, policies and labour – has resulted in an island-city of immense contrasts, with monumental modern buildings standing alongside strongly differentiated neighbourhoods with their dilapidated 1960s apartment blocks in places like Sissimiut. During the decades following the Second World War, standard houses and blocks of flats dominated the urban landscape in Greenland, due to the need to house a lot of citizens within a limited amount of space.

At the end of the 1980s, a new economic reality began to emerge. Previously the state had owned almost 90% of all houses on the <u>transferable housing market</u> aimed at the middle-income groups. The system was however proving to be simply too expensive to maintain and had to be changed.

The new system focused on the **housing co-operative**. Here the middle-income group could become house owners – with a little

---

[20] Adam Grydehoj [University of Prince Edward Island, Canada]: extract from article in Island Studies Journal, Nov 2014

help from **Home Rule**.[21] Of paramount importance was the fact that building maintenance was no longer the responsibility of the public administration. The Home Rule Government supported the establishment of **cooperative ownership** with up to 50% of the costs financed through special loans.[22]

At the beginning of the new millennium, **a new and financially stronger middle-income group began to dominate the housing market in a number of towns, and most visibly in the capital, Nuuk**. Here for the first time a whole zone was established, comprising only privately owned houses and flats **operating more or less on market terms.**

The 2009 referendum resulted in Greenland having self-governing status and administering its own territory and

---

[21] Following a referendum in **Greenland** where the majority favoured a higher degree of autonomy, **home rule** was granted by the Parliament of Denmark in 1979.

[22] In the UK we have had housing associations taking over from local authorities in some areas in providing and managing large-scale **'social housing' stock**. And we have Government legislating for the sale of local authority homes to their long-standing tenants for a hugely discounted price ['Right to buy']. And more recently we have had the Government offering to provide [say] 10% of the deposit on new-build transferable ownership homes for take-up by first-time home buyers. Of course, the UK has had leasehold blocks of flats for many decades, though the lessee is in truth no more than a subservient tenant of the freehold owner of the block, and with a tenancy for an assured period of 50/99+ years, along with a contractual obligation to pay an ever-growing service charge annually. **So the Greenland cooperative model is one which allows the resident to have a share of the equity, with the island's Government retaining the remaining share.** This can to a degree be likened to the UK model whereby certain housing associations – as 'developers' - allow qualifying residents to purchase an increasingly large stake in the equity of a new-build property, whilst paying the housing association a rent for the balance owned by the association.

resources. But on the world's largest island, land ownership is complex and unorthodox. **All land is owned by Greenlandic municipalities and leased for private or commercial purposes when required. However, only the foundations and any above-ground construction are owned by the lessee; the land below it is not.** One observer described the result as being *'an urban landscape devoid of fences and walls. Housing and public buildings populate the landscape as if dropped from the sky.'[23]*

There is a minimum distance of 10 metres between buildings for fire safety, but otherwise towns and hamlets have grown organically. Access to the coast and the impact of local topography are the key design determinants. Stepping out of your front door means, literally, stepping into public space.

Most Greenlandic housing takes the form of archetypal, gable-roofed timber dwellings, predominantly clad in timber and so reflecting tradition, timber's inherent malleability and weathering qualities and a long established timber supply line from Denmark.

Colourful facades still prevail, and this colouring initially had a more pragmatic purpose, communicating a settlement's functions over long distances to passing fishermen. Supply stores, churches and schools were painted red, hospitals yellow and municipal buildings blue. During the Second World War, another layer of information was added. A number and letter combination known only to the Allies was painted on rooftops in

---

[23] Clearly the observer seemed preconditioned into accepting that `an Englishman's home is his castle' and may not have read Robert Frost's poem about stone walls and peoples' preoccupation with wanting to cut themselves off from their neighbours! We all need space between our `territories' just as do all animals and birds, but just how far should we take this?

order to identify a particular settlement from the air while confusing enemy aircraft.

The process of developing a growing housing market operating, more or less, on market terms is being replicated in the four new 'administrative' towns, one in each of the four municipalities created in 2009, and perhaps in a few other villages.

Nuuk today - both at the centre and on the periphery – is very much involved in economic relationships with other Greenlandic settlements and with Denmark. The Greenlandic settlement owes much of its present-day character to urban design processes akin to those we see manifested across Western Europe, North America, etc. Capital generates capital through development, and Nuuk is no exception. What we witness today is a form of a 'lowish-rise' `internationalist' development in the new residential areas of the city, though partially reflecting the Scandinavian traditions of the Danish who are playing a key rôle in this expansion. And the marinas with their yachts are a further expression of this changing character, this growing affluence.

Greenland has its wealthy families, and some of this wealth has now been invested in large, private houses of some 200 square metres floor area, which in Greenland amounts to a luxury house. In all of Greenland's towns, specific areas have now come to be characterized by such properties, with a few in the smaller towns and up to fifty plus in Nuuk. From the 1950s there has been a small and highly profitable market for these houses, with supply now balancing demand. People living in these 'luxury' houses include successful entrepreneurs, shrimp trawler owners, directors in the state owned organisations, top civil servants, and politicians. It is impossible to say whether the housing bubble in Greenland will burst. If it does, it will impact a large group of middle-income citizens, but it will probably not really affect the exclusive little group of housing matadors, who have benefited enormously from the housing boom aided by the Home Rule system.

Looking beyond Greenland, it is striking to observe the current state of the housing market in, for example, **the high north of Canada. In Nunavut and in Nunavik the housing market structure shows remarkable similarities to that of Greenland some 40 or 50 years ago.** It will therefore be interesting to see how the housing market in these parts of the Arctic will develop in the years to come.

Nevertheless, Nuuk has had its share of false starts. As with many of the blocks built in the UK, the `notorious' **Block P in Nuuk** has now been demolished as a failure. The construction of **Block P** in the 1960s was a response to a strategic decision by Danish Government noted above but arguably divorced from those directly affected - **to decant and rehouse many of the populace from Greenland's coastal fishing villages.** The construction of UK's poorly designed social housing blocks was perhaps a vote-catching decision, though the thinking behind Block P was possibly related to a misguided notion of `social reform' whereby the Danish instigators and designers did not start with any real notion of a connection with the lives and culture of the Greenlanders it was built to house.

New, small-scale shopping development at Maniitsoq

As in the UK, the blocks have proved to be a failure, both socially and economically. Block P's history demonstrated that society/community could not be remodelled instantly, Utopian-style, by the construction of a series of large-scale blocks of flats. Greenlandic society has developed over hundreds of years and was based on a pattern of life that is now being superseded at a quickening pace. Industrialisation of fish-processing, the emergence of new types of work and the concentration of the population in a number of larger towns have given rise to family-destabilization. Depression, poverty, alcoholism and dysfunctional parental homes have sadly been linked to the high incidence of suicide on the island.

For a long while, discussion of suicide issues has been **taboo** among the population, especially the youth who had to endure it at home. Youth projects have encouraged open-discussion of the subject and this has helped them to both address the subject head-on and seek new ways of dealing with it. But has Greenland's government – or indeed Britain's -learned the lessons of Block P and its many more British equivalents?

I am indebted to David Garcia of the Bartlett School of Architecture, University of London, whose analysis of the history behind Blok P , published in the UK's *Architectural Review*[24], holds true for much of the high-density social housing in Greenland and elsewhere.

The block was built from 1965 to 1966 as part of the Danish Government's **Folketinget** Programme – that ran from 1953 - which set out to modernise and urbanise Greenland's infrastructure by decanting the population from those coastal settlements that it deemed 'unprofitable, unhealthy and unmodern.'

Even today, large, so-called 'Soviet-style'[25] apartment blocks loom behind what – in retrospect - is considered a misguided attempt on the part of the Danes in the 1950s and 1960s to urbanise the country's population. It was an attempt at rapid social transformation that the Inuits were unprepared for and had little if any control over. When it was built it was the largest building construction in the Kingdom of Denmark. The size and

---

[24] `*View from Nuuk, Greenland*', Architectural Review, 2th March, 2012
[25] UK business-journalists' terminology

floor plan of the apartments were described as entirely unsuitable for the Inuit lifestyle, with narrow doorways making it difficult - or sometimes impossible - to enter and exit wearing thick cold weather clothing, and common European style wardrobes were too small to store fishing gear. This gear was then stored on the balconies, blocking fire exits and creating a security hazard. During the first years there were minor problems with coagulated blood clogging up the drainage, stemming from the fishermen using the only available reasonable place to carve up their catch: the bathtubs. Five stories high, and with 64 apartments on each floor, its length extended to over 200 metres, cutting right across the city of Nuuk in an east-west direction. Unsurprisingly, Blok P was not viewed very favourably by a sizeable proportion the local populace, and it was even presented to visiting tourists as being "so depressing as to be almost an attraction in itself". Containing about 320 flats, it accommodated about 1 in every 100 of Greenland's population.

The block – the largest residential building not only in Nuuk but in Greenland as a whole - was demolished in its entirety on the 19th October, 2012 by the national authorities. The municipality had instigated the staged demolition of a number of similar structures, the so-called Bloks A,B,C,D,E,E,G,H,I,J,K and L, which also had a central location. The residents were mainly 'decanted'[26] to housing in Qinngorput, and Blok P was dismantled in five stages, starting in 2011, with the final stage of land clearing and handover in 2014.

The city then held workshops for future development of the area in its **2024** plan. Parallel to this, both the national- and the local

---

[26] To reluctantly use an expression familiar to local authorities in the UK …….

authorities have started to develop new plans for the area. The local architectural practice **TNTnuuk**, alongside Norway's Tromsø-based **Dahl & Uhre** architects, was commissioned to develop this project. There are no concrete plans yet for the 'permanent' redevelopment of the Block P site; however since July 2013 the city has developed an interim community building project on the site, called the 'Nuuk Playground', designed to address the needs of the community.

Greenland's Inuit population seems withdrawn, especially by comparison with the communities of the West Indies, especially the Eastern Caribbean. To the outsider, they seem at first sight to be shy, introvert, compared to the extrovert Antiguans and Barbadians. Part of this is probably to do with the language barrier between the Inuits and the tourist visitors, though with structural changes to the island's economy, greater emphasis will no doubt be placed on overcoming this. The West Indians have a British Colonial slave heritage, with English having been the 'official' language for several hundred years. It will be interesting to see whether Danish and/or English become the second/third languages of the Inuits as their dealings with the outside trading world grow.

THE NUUK MASTERPLAN

In April, 2011 an exhibition was held to present a new Master Plan for Nuuk, and the commentary that accompanied the proposals remarked that:

*"For better or worse, **the Tuujuk and Block P developments** [then pending demolition] stand as symbols of a time of great social and cultural challenges ...... The ties between the residents and the energy that exists, is strong. After 40 years, Blok P with its 135*

*apartments and 50 residential dwellings is due for demolition, and Block A – L in Tuujuk with 156 apartments will be undergoing a phased demolition over a period of years. The problem is simple: **as time has passed, the housing has become outdated.**[27] In the process of rebuilding the areas, a number of important questions must be asked: What qualities survive today and what new possibilities and qualities should we aim to generate? What kind of life and environment should we strive to create? What type of town should it be? What role could the district play in Nuuk's overall development? In short: What kind of capital city should we aim for? Our response these questions must embody the acquisition of new experiences ….. lessons arising from Blok P and Tuujuk need to be learnt and understood. (In short) our existing thought-models need to be re-thought."*

All this poses these questions:

- How empathetic was the Block P design-group to the needs and aspirations of the people who initially moved into Blok P? What cultural aspects did the designers and the residents share?

- In addition, did members the team behind the 2011 Plan share any of the life-experiences, values and aspirations of the Greenlanders who seek good quality, affordable housing?

---

[27] Given the public expenditure on constructing the blocks and the relatively short time that they stood, politicians needed to find a justification for demolishing them that would be palatable to the tax-payers, especially in Denmark!

Striving to reconcile tradition with progress, Greenland's capital Nuuk is experiencing a dire housing shortage that is likely to intensify.

With a population of just over 56,000 inhabiting the world's largest island, Greenland is the least dense nation on the planet, **yet lack of housing is 'endemic'.** The current demand for housing in Nuuk, with a population of just over 15,000, has generated

Block P and subsequent re-development ideas

waiting lists of up to 17 years. If plots, flats and allotments are contested by several claims, ownership is decided by lottery.

It is claimed that

- this lack of housing is largely due to lack of investment;
- that It is prohibitively expensive to build in Greenland;
- and that all construction materials have to be imported.

So it is still said to be cheaper to prefabricate in Denmark (or even China) and transport the structure to Greenland than to build locally. It would be fair to say that the suggested large scale use of the local granite would be totally impractical, though its use on a small scale would help link new buildings with their landscape context.

It is further alleged that no attempt has been made to challenge or explore alternative ways of building here,[28] though, strangely, no reference is made as to the degree to which local training colleges are able to equip the local populace with the skills needed to build homes economically.   Perceptions of major public investment costs are, however, often fraught with subjectivity.[29]

---

[28] There have been similar claims in the UK, where it has been suggested that a far greater use of modular prefabricated composite [steel] units would help solve the nation's housing shortage. Imaginative building design, combined with good contextual design could work in both the UK and Greenland, with mass production helping to bring about affordability. Given Greenland's rocky topography and scarcity of level ground, this approach might be advantageous.
Land ownership lies at the root of change in the UK, the challenge being that house builders are amassing large land-banks and producing ever smaller, more tightly packed brick houses. The UK's mid-20C New Town Development Corporations had powers to compulsory purchase land and create unique communities, and a variant might offer a model for breaking free from the present vendor-led determinants.
[29]   Small-scale   disability-friendly   public-sphere   pedestrian-preference/public-space   schemes   are   considered   'exceptional

One of the most important current housing policy issues in Greenland is the future of the land on which 'Block P' sat in the centre of Nuuk. Even though Nuuk is a relatively small city, central plots are attractive for shopping, offices and middle-class housing. In such a context, the vacated 'Blok P' site represents an almost ideal location for redevelopment.

One of the main elements of the redevelopment process thus far has been a major proposal-exhibition and guaranteed public involvement. Interestingly enough, the Norwegian Ministry of Foreign Affairs contributed 300 000 NOK to this part of the project. Knut Erik Dahl from **Dahl & Uhre architects** explained that this Norwegian Government support related to the 'indigenous people' dimension of this project and to the exchange of skills and knowledge on the topic of 'the Arctic City', while noting that Norwegian efforts to develop policies for the High North are also relevant.

In total, Greenland has almost 27 000 housing-units including 7, 200 dwellings. A total of 274 new homes were constructed in Greenland in 2009. Of these, 136 were built in Nuuk. Of the new dwellings, 179 are publicly owned. The Greenland Housing Association Ltd (A/S Inissiaatileqatigiiffik INI) manages and maintains about 12 000 public/social rental dwellings on behalf of both the Government of Greenland and many of the municipalities. Just over 16 000 of Greenland's approximately 57 000 inhabitants live in Nuuk. In Greenland's Nordic neighbours,

---

expenditure' items across much of the UK whereas on mainland Western Europe, civic pride is the norm, and the implementation of large-scale schemes of a high specification has been taken for granted for decades.

Iceland, 33% of the population live in the capital, Reykjavik; and more than 60% if you include the suburbs.

On the **Faroe Islands**, the population is almost comparable, with about 5,000 fewer Faroese than Greenlanders. Here, only 38% live in **Torshavn**, the capital, but the islands have a better infrastructure with roads and tunnels, enabling more people to live outside the capital and commute to work. **In Greenland, there are no roads between the towns.** Here, you must sail or fly between towns and villages and, like the rest of the world, only a few people return to the smaller settlements, once they have lived in a town. Thus Nuuk will continue to grow and if the predictions of the "Capital Strategy" prove to be true, a lot of planning and preparation will be necessary before the city has capacity for 30,000 inhabitants, the equivalent of 55% of Greenland's population.

Klaus Georg Hansen[30] believes that

Greenland's bigger towns are providing examples of how a unique Greenlandic architecture is beginning to take shape. He considers that, as with their ancestors, modern-day Greenlanders have a special relationship with nature, and this is finding its way onto architects' drawing boards.

This is a huge step forward. The people for whom these houses were meant were unable however to provide any financing of their own. Therefore, loans, which did not need to be repaid for thirty years were introduced. And although the system seemed to work well for decades, it was ultimately concluded that those

---

[30] Head of the Interior Division, The Premier's Office, Greenland

who were unable to pay the loan at the outset were unlikely to be able to pay it thirty years later. Subsequently most of these loans were simply written off.

The issues surrounding modern-day housing in Greenland are in many respects typical in the Western World, if not the world as a whole.[31] Private land ownership in Greenland is forbidden, a prohibition that has shaped the Arctic country's housing market, differing dramatically from, for example, that of the United States. Nearly half of Greenlanders, for instance, live in state-managed rentals, while 99 percent of Americans live in privately owned or managed units. But Greenland offers an interesting case study for those housing reformers of a politically left persuasion who have recently expressed renewed interest in public housing.

Following World War II, both the U.S. and Greenland embarked on ambitious programmes of public-housing construction. In Greenland, this process was managed by Danes from far off Copenhagen, sent with a mission to relocate native Greenlanders from Inuit fishing villages to urbanized public-housing campuses. The program improved the living standards of the Inuit migrants, who often left wood-and-peat houses for modern structures where they enjoyed running water, modern sewage, and electricity for the first time. But on a deeper level, it also transformed Inuit life: the new housing clashed with native folkways by imposing Danish lifestyles and social structures.

Construction of Blok P in Nuuk began in 1965, a 5-story monstrosity that stretched 64 apartments wide, **Blok P** was said

---

[31]Nolan Grey has summarised the principal issues surrounding housing in Greenland today, but interestingly, **from an American perspective**. He is a city planner and contributor to 'Market Urbanism.'

to have been an eyesore from the very beginning, and not even remotely conducive to Inuit ways of life.The project's modern amenities were a boon to the new residents, but problems soon abounded, particularly with unit designs. Small closets, built to European preferences, couldn't support the coats and undergarments needed for Artic life. Narrow doorways and corridors, meantime, made walking in bulky coats burdensome. With no dedicated space to clean fish—a staple of the Inuit diet—residents started preparing their catches in bathtubs, which clogged building pipes. Nature only added to the trouble: annual spring melts revived the bog, creating a moat around Blok P. To top it off, segregation characterized the building, with Danish migrants clustered away from the Inuit majority. ***Imagined Space*** was a project about "Blok P" in Nuuk, Greenland, and the people who lived there, including the short period leading up to its demolition. Blok P was the largest residential building in all of Greenland, and the largest building in Nuuk. It contained around 150 apartments and it is said that approximately 1% of the total population of Greenland lived in this building when it was built. When it was demolished, all the inhabitants were relocated, along with a lifetime of memories. Many of the inhabitants had been living there for most of their lives. At the time of the project, the Blok had become a ghost town with only few families left, and the aim of Imagined Space was to portray some of the people who had lived, or were still living there. The aim was to end up with an honest document of the lived life in within a historic apartment block in Nuuk, based on interviews, sound field recordings, photos and video.

By the mid-2000s, Blok P had fallen into disrepair. In 2009, Greenlandic officials closed the facility, celebrating their decision with a table-length cake designed to mimic the apartment's conspicuous length. Residents were offered new public units in

Qinngorput, an expansion on the far side of town, though few made the move. By 2014, the infamous housing project was gone.

Greenlanders secured home rule from Denmark in 1979, allowing the island to manage its internal affairs. Autonomy had big implications for housing, with a new government quickly undertaking a privatization programme. This endeavour, which attempted to move maintenance costs off the books, granted Greenlanders ownership over their own homes and encouraged renters to form private housing cooperatives.

Here the middle-income group could become house (co)owners – with a little help from Home Rule. Of paramount importance here was the fact that building maintenance was no longer the responsibility of the Government or the local authorities. So a small private housing market has emerged since the 1980s, although many Greenlanders still write monthly cheques made out to the state.

One can make a case that Greenland is most suited to public housing because the population largely lacks the resources to cover the high costs of imported construction materials and labor. To that end, the country continues to build hundreds of units each year, with so-called 'cookie-cutter blocks'[32] still springing up in vacant plots on the outskirts of many Greenlandic towns.

---

[32] This Americanism refers to bland rectangular blocks with monotonous, undistinguished elevations reflecting the lack of care inherent in the design of the apartments.

CHAPTER FOUR:

IN SEARCH OF ECONOMIC- AND POLITICAL INDEPENDENCE

Oil is a fossil fuel; nevertheless, there is a body of opinion in Greenland that believes that it might benefit economically from the oil-reserves below its seabed basins, along with the oceanic fish-stocks and the on-shore uranium/mineral/Rare Earth resources. Fish stocks depend largely upon the availability of plankton, a suitable marine environment and effective international control systems to prevent over-fishing and pollution of the sea and fjords. Uranium extraction depends foremost upon international acceptability of nuclear energy - with enormous health-hazard centring upon the safe disposal of radioactive spent fuel - as an alternative energy source to crude oil, a fossil fuel. And oil prospecting depends on the size of the reserves and the viability of retrieving them without prejudice to the cleanliness of the earth's oceans and their marine-stock. In Greenland, the national government, which is now in control of subsurface rights [once held by Denmark] is often caught up in messy mining politics. Yet Greenland is often cited as a treasure house of minerals from rare earths to uranium, rubies, gold, copper and silver. The deposits of Kuannersuit [Kvanefjeld] in southern Greenland are thought to contain up to 2 million tonnes of rare earth minerals, which, if they were to be exploited, would offer a counterbalance to the global production dominance enjoyed by Chinese producers. China controls around 90% of the world's rare earth metal market and the US imports over 90% of its domestic needs from China, principally to satisfy the smartphone market.

FISHING

In Greenland and the Faroe Islands, more than 90% of the total value of exports is generated by fishing. By way of comparison, fishing constituted almost half of the total value of exports from Iceland in 2016. The fishing sector is thus a critical part of the Arctic region. The vast majority of trade in goods to and from the Arctic relies on maritime transport. Addressing the challenge of converting maritime transport from fossil fuels to renewable energy is therefore a central aspect of forward-thinking.

URANIUM PROSPECTING AND MINING

The possibility of uranium mining in Greenland was first raised **when the island's parliament reversed a longstanding "zero tolerance" policy toward uranium extraction in 2013, clearing the way for the mining of REEs and uranium**, (which co-exist at the **Kvanefjeld** site). That decision, however, sparked off a prolonged legal battle between Denmark's Copenhagen and Greenland's capital, Nuuk, which was ultimately resolved in early 2016, so allowing the **Kvanefjeld** project to go forward. At the heart of the dispute has been the political relationship between the Kingdom of Denmark and Greenland as part of that Kingdom, though with substantial political autonomy. The **2009 Self-Government Act** - which specified the powers of the Greenland government and included control over economic affairs - **left Denmark with oversight of the island's defence and foreign affairs.**

Uranium is almost entirely used for generating electricity, though fundamental changes are underway. As of January 2015, **437 commercial nuclear reactors were linked to the grid worldwide,** generating 377 GWe and consuming about 56,600 tons of uranium annually.

South Greenland stands out as the most uranium-rich province in Greenland, where the best uranium prospects are located with the help of airborne gamma-spectrometry, stream sediment sampling and stream-water geochemistry. **The uranium potential in Greenland is relatively high**, with – at the time of writing - one very large deposit already being moving toward production (pending application and approval). Existing evidence from surveys - combined with field investigations - points to **South Greenland** as the most prospective region for additional hidden or unrecognised intrusive-type uranium occurrences. Favourable geological settings for **unconformity-related uranium mineralisation** are constantly being identified, suggesting a potential for the occurrence of such deposits.

oooooooooOOOOOOOooooooooo

OIL AND NATURAL GAS DRILLING

Prospecting for crude oil has been taking place off Greenland's coast for at least a decade, and the Greenlandic Government has been placing great store on this potential source of wealth for the island. After all, Norway has become super-rich on the back of its off-shore oil production revenues, and Russia has been making great strides to similarly enrichen its economy, including exporting the crude oil.

The area above the Arctic Circle is underlain by sedimentary basins and continental shelves that hold enormous oil- and natural gas reserves. Most of this area is relatively poorly explored thus far; however, the **United States Geological Survey** estimates that the Arctic contains approximately 13 percent of the world's undiscovered conventional oil resources and about 30 percent of its undiscovered conventional natural gas resources. It is about the same geographic size as the African continent - about 6% of Earth's surface area - **yet it holds an estimated 22 percent of Earth's oil and natural gas resources. Most of the Arctic area resource is natural gas** and that on the Asian side of the Arctic area has the highest proportion of natural gas and natural gas liquids.

Offshore exploration in the Arctic currently targets oil instead of

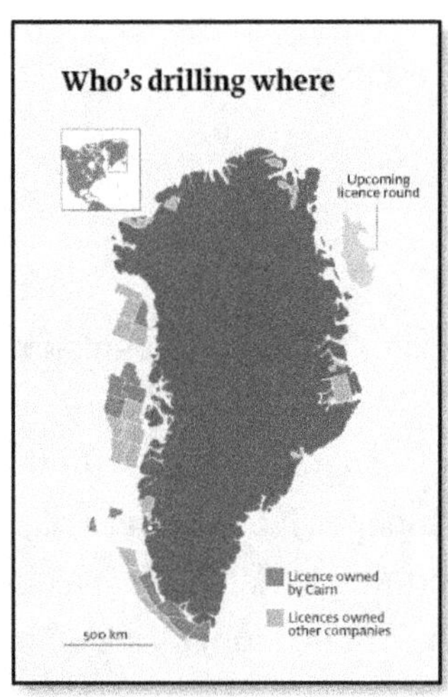

Map of initial oil-field licence allocation around Greenland

natural gas. The relative ease of transport is what causes companies to favour oil. Where ice-free water is available, oil can be produced from a well, placed on a ship and transported to refineries such as those in the UK. It can also be transported by pipeline; however, the construction of pipelines in the Arctic represents projects of enormous difficulty and scale.

Natural gas is much more difficult to transport to market. It has a much lower energy density and must be super-cooled to a liquid for movement by sea. This requires a large, complex and expensive facility that takes several years to commission. Pipeline construction for natural gas encounters the same expenses and problems as those required to transport oil.

Yet it seems that there has been **no commercial oil retrieval** despite the expenditure of billions of pounds sterling/dollars by the world's bigger oil corporations. Just a few years on from being granted licenses to undertake prospect-drilling, only two of the

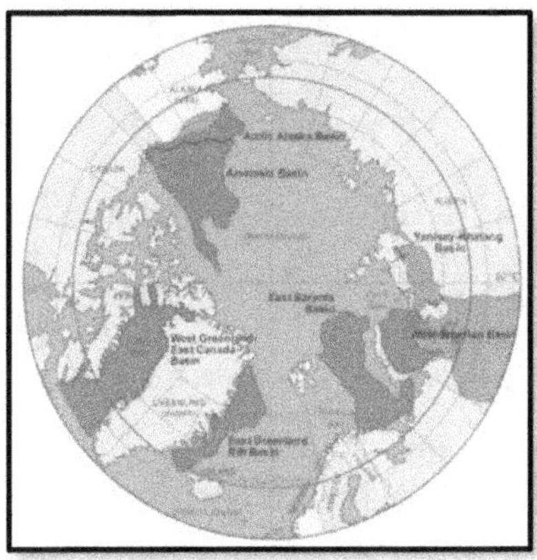

ARCTIC OIL AND NATURAL GAS PROVINCES: The US Geological Survey estimates that 87%+ of the Arctic's oil and natural gas resource (about 360 billion barrels oil equivalent) is located in seven Arctic basin provinces: Amerasian, Arctic Alaska, East Barents, **East Greenland Rift, West Greenland-East Canada,** West Siberian, and the Yenisey-Khatanga. Map by Geology.com and MapResources.

four oil wells that the Scottish oil company **Cairn** had been granted a licence to sink, were actually drilled, with no meaningful oil removed. Tens of millions of pounds sterling were lost in the effort and the Greenlandic Government's dream of reaping oil-revenues that would propel it further along its path to greater independence seemed to have been thwarted. The 2008 study of the basins of the Arctic Ocean by the **US Geological Survey** estimated that three 'provinces' off the coast

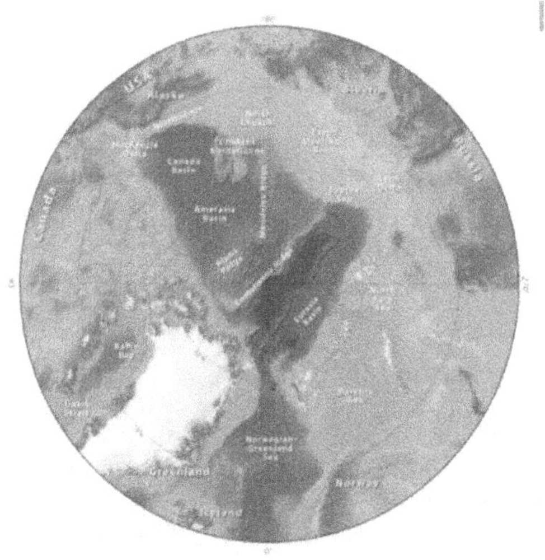

Map of Arctic ridges and basins. The Arctic Basin contains a high proportion of continental crust on its flor; there was a significant deposition of dead plankton and algae settling on the basin floor, to be covered by sediment from eroded mountains and squashed by the increasing weight of the sediment to warm and turn into oil and gas. These in turn migrated upwards through the rock fissures to form reservoirs that we now tap.

of Greenland could together yield up to 52 billion barrels of oil equivalent (which includes natural gas) – as much as has been drilled out of the North Sea in the past 40 years. This statistic caught the attention of companies including **ExxonMobil and Royal Dutch Shell**, and explains Scotland's **Cairn Energy** presence. **Kuupik Kleist**, Greenland's prime minister and leader of the country's Inuit Ataqatigiit party, noted the potential reserve figures, seeing oil as a possible route to Greenland's economic independence.

 'Self-governing' since 2009, Greenland remains a dependency of Denmark, and each year the island receives an annual subsidy of about DKK3.2bn (£375m) from Denmark, which helps fund social services. The export of fish brings in revenues of about DKK2bn (£235m). Everything else is imported.

FOSSIL FUELS –V– THE ENVIRONMENT

That said, the irony of Greenland becoming a major producer of fossil-fuel hydrocarbons, and contributing to the climate change that is helping to melt its own glaciers, is not lost on Mr Kleist, **although the root of the problem, he says, lies in the failure of the rest of the world to curb its appetite for energy. "The western press is focusing on whether Greenland should or should not exploit its natural resources," he says. "They don't focus on the consumption of energy."** The country's potential hydrocarbon wealth "holds a very big economic potential," says Kleist. But as a fossil fuel, oil has to be considered as a transitional resource because of its negative environmental impact and the growing importance of electric vehicles.

The mention of potential oil drilling in Greenland's territorial waters sparked off Greenpeace's 'rapid reaction' protestors and since then there has been an ongoing campaign by the wider protest movement, supported by other sympathetic organizations. For international climate-change campaigners, drilling for oil and gas in the Arctic is the final insult. "We are drawing a line in the ice," says Nick Young, a volunteer and blogger from New Zealand. "If we see the melting of the ice caps as an opportunity to drill for oil, then what hope is there?"

Sea ice is melting as quickly as the accelerating advance of Global Warming, and **open-water seasons now last longer in Greenland**; the major oil companies are all now preparing to move into areas where, it is said, a spill would not only be almost impossible to clean up, but could take years to even control. Yet, conservationists increasingly stress that it is only a matter of time before a catastrophic spill devastates some of the least polluted waters in the world. **The crucial difference is that any spillage around Greenland would not be offset by any evaporation because of the cooler climate and water-temperatures.**

According to **Greenpeace**, a blowout of the kind that BP experienced in the Gulf of Mexico would be even more devastating off Greenland, where whales, polar bears, seals and fish live in abundance. A relief-well might not be completed in the same drilling season, leading to oil gushing out unchecked for up to two years. Oil would probably become trapped under the ice, making it impossible to remove.

"No oil company is remotely prepared for a major spill in the Arctic", says WWF[33]. Yet the worrying ecological implications of this probably cut little ice with the likes of oil-giants BP; for them, the vast area above the Arctic Circle has become the oil industry's

---

[33] World Wide Fund for Nature

new frontier, offering potentially billions of barrels of oil from deep offshore wells in return for the huge technical, safety and financial risks. The likes of BP are now focused upon an area on the north-eastern side of Greenland.

At around the time when licences were granted, the leader of Greenland's **Organisation of Fishermen and Hunters**, said that he was against offshore oil development, because "you cannot control environmental conditions". He worried about what a spill would do to his members' livelihoods. The president of Greenland's **Inuit Circumpolar Council** (ICC), the international non-government organisation that represents around 150,000 Inuits of Alaska, Canada, Chukotka (Russia) and Greenland, was said to be outwardly more conciliatory,

Gazprom's Prirazlomnaya Rig.
Credit: Gazprom

He said the government needed to take into account "the view of the public society ….. (and instead) to be focused on emphasizing "a human dimension" to the debate about drilling in the Arctic, not just the environmental one.[34]

So Greenland is not alone in trying to deal with this oil v environment contradiction, and can benefit from Norway's experience, the latter having already reaped significant financial gain from oil drilling before performing a 'U-Turn'. The UK's *Guardian* newspaper reported that the largest party in Norway's parliament has delivered a significant blow to the country's huge oil industry by withdrawing support for explorative drilling off the **Lofoten islands in the Arctic**, which are considered a natural wonder.

The political move created a large parliamentary majority **against** oil exploration in the sensitive offshore area, illustrating growing opposition to the polluting fossil fuel, which has made Norway one of the world's most affluent.

The newspaper reported that Norway currently pumps out over 1.6 million barrels of oil a day from its offshore operations. Norway's largest oil producer, the state-controlled company Equinor ASA, has said gaining access to oil supplies in **Lofoten** is essential for the country to maintain production levels. It is thought there are between one- and three billion barrels of oil beneath the seabed off the Lofoten archipelago. The area had already been kept off limits for years by Norway's coalition government through various political deals.

---

[34] 25/03/2020: Author's reflection based on recent events in the north of England: Yes, fracking for shale-gas using subterranean explosives might provide some employment if it becomes commercially viable, but what damage will the vibrations and shock waves do to peoples' homes in the vicinity of the fracking process? The UK Government has recently had a change of heart and is temporarily stopping the fracking.

Norway's government fairly recently gave the go-ahead for its $1trillion (£760bn) Oil Fund – the world's largest sovereign wealth fund – to invest in renewable energy projects not listed on stock markets. Billions are earmarked for wind- and solar power projects, demonstrating that wealth accumulated through fossil fuels is being redirected towards future profits in renewable energy. Greater numbers of industries and countries have begun fossil fuel divestment strategies, citing future risks to their business and economic models. Whilst it continued to support the oil industry as a very important contributor to the country's economy, the Norwegian Government wants oil firms in the country to commit to a deadline for making all operations emissions free. Furthermore, Norway's Oil Fund said it would no longer invest in 134 companies which explore for oil and gas, but would retain stakes in large oil firms including BP and Shell, which have renewable energy divisions.'

In the *Guardian*'s scrutiny of the Arctic, the newspaper investigated **the impact of oil drilling** in the Alaskan part of the Arctic.

"The Arctic .... a last great unprotected wilderness, safe subsistence lifestyle has survived in harmony with nature for thousands of years..... It is here that Shell Oil plans to drill for oil, pulling the detonator on a carbon bomb which eventually could spray 150bn tonnes of carbon dioxide into the atmosphere.

The irony is that drilling is only possible because manmade climate change is already causing this region to grow warmer twice as fast as the rest of the planet, (with the) melting ice making these huge reserves of oil and gas more accessible. ......
No wonder some fear a new cold war. **Now a British presence is being established in Alaska by the Anglo Dutch Shell Group, though it is NOT one which is welcome by all, especially some of those who live in the tumble of wooden homes that hug the shoreline.....** Rosemary Ahtuangaruak being one of them. The

self-styled environmental justice adviser is among other things a stalwart defender of **Inupiat culture**.

"I work with nonprofit organisations that want to protect the Arctic Ocean and wilderness areas. It's about raising the importance of health, tradition and culture in the venues of those (Shell and others) who want to change our lands and waters," she says, one eye on three grandchildren she is minding.

"It's about the (any future oil) spill. They cannot clear up in icy conditions that we have for eight or nine months of the year. The ecosystem renewal, needed for the many different animals that migrate here, is important because we are feeding our families from the ocean. We must keep this environment pristine. Ahtuangaruak is convinced the subsistence way of life practised by the Inupiat could be extinguished for future generations in the event of oil pollution.... "

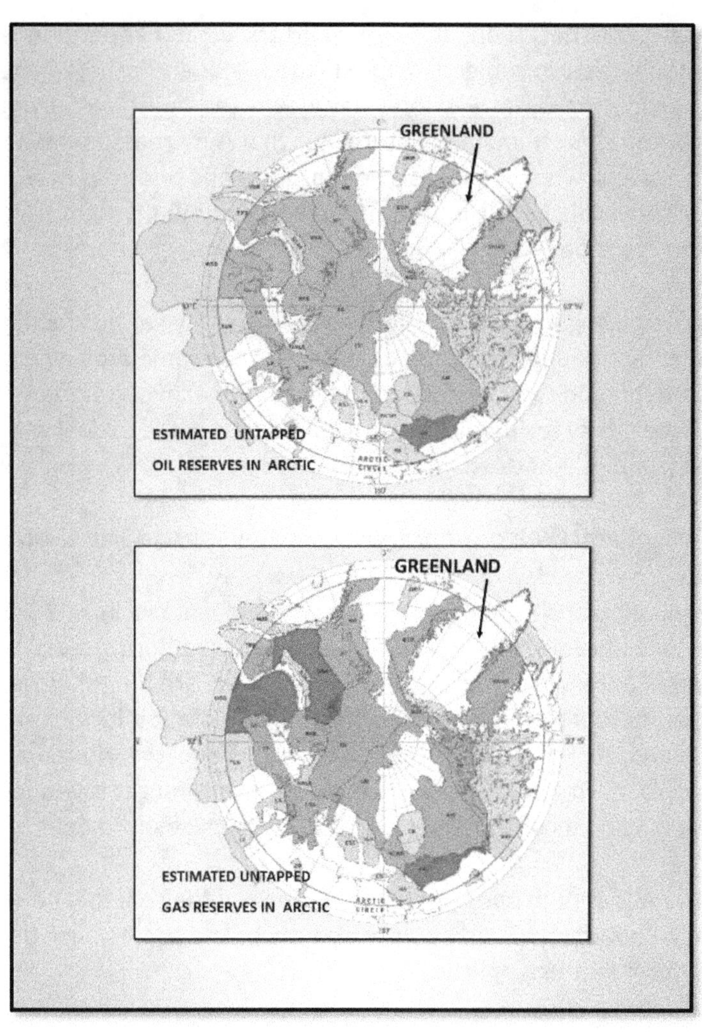

ESTIMATED UNDISCOVERED OIL
Dark Green = >10 billion barrels; Medium
Green = 1–10, light = <1

She says she has seen at close quarters what happens in a community that is subject to an oil rush….. BP and others have been producing oil at Prudhoe Bay down the coast east from Barrow for more than half century. But that is no reassurance to Ahtuangaruak who worked as a health aide – and briefly as mayor of the small village of Nuiqsut, an Inupiat community right next door to Prudhoe Bay.

"I learned living in Nuiqsut; there are some really serious health impacts that happen to our people living in the same area where this is happening (oil extraction): cancer rates have gone up … acute sensitivity to chemicals and even suicides. I had to deal with the sick babies. That's why I argue so hard now."

In a recent article on on-shore gas extraction[35], Irena Slav wrote:

"Greenland plans to auction onshore oil and gas blocks in 2021 with two Chinese state majors already expressing interest in bidding, Reuters reports…….. CNPC and CNOOC are the (Chinese) companies that will likely make offers for exploration in western Greenland, in the area of the Disko Island and the Nuussuaq Peninsula, as Greenland seeks to increase its oil and gas revenues by opening up its onshore resources besides its offshore ones.

The island's deputy energy minister, Jorn Skov Nielsen, told news agency Reuters " ……..It's a new approach. We are moving the short-term strategy of licensing onshore."

According to a 2008 <u>estimate</u> by the U.S. Geological Survey, Greenland—the world's largest island—could contain as much as 17.53 billion barrels of crude as well as 148.21 trillion cubic feet

------

[35] "Greenland to launch on-shore oil-gas tender in 2021", on 'Oilprice.com'

[about 4.8 trillion cubic metres] of natural gas. Including natural gas liquid resources, the total hydrocarbon estimate for the island was almost 52 billion barrels of oil equivalent.

Yet China is not really the favorite candidate of Copenhagen: the news agency recalls recent concern expressed by both the Danish and the U.S. governments over a proposal by Chinese companies to take part in financing and building airports in Greenland. Ultimately, Greenland quenched the concern by picking Denmark to help it to upgrade two local airports.

Still, the autonomous government is naturally interested in pursuing business links with Chinese companies, which have the financial resources and the demand to potentially ensure a long-term market for Greenland's oil and gas. According to Nielsen, Greenland's government expressed its intention to set up an office in Beijing at the time.

The island itself, however, has a lot greener plans for its own energy needs: it currently sources 70 percent of its energy from hydropower and will aim to raise this to 100 percent by 2030.

ALUMINIUM SMELTING

Advanced plans for the Alcoa aluminium smelting plant in the **Qeqqata** municipality have been in place for a good number of years. **Maniitsoq**, Greenland's second-largest town, is one of the proposed locations, alongside the municipal centre in **Sisimiut**. The plant would provide employment for 600–700 people, or more than 10 percent of the population. As it is a vital decision for the town, wide public consultations were carried out in 2008–2010 by both the town authorities and the Government of Greenland in order to address potential environmental and social concerns.

A hydroelectric power plant at the **Majorqaq** river source would yield an estimated energy output of 1,000 gigawatt-hours per year. Combined with the second plant near **Kangerlussuatsiaq Fjord** with 3,170 gigawatt-hours per year, the energy would be sufficient to power the aluminium plant near Maniitsoq. The ultimate decision as to the location of the plant has not yet been taken.

Fuel costs and local construction costs are the principal determinants of smelting plant location. Greenland's Government has said that the decision to site an Alcoa[36] smelting plant in Greenland depended upon the plant being 'competitive on a global scale' with countries such as China in relation to construction labour costs and ongoing running costs. This in practise means selling energy and labour to Alcoa as cheaply as possible and providing Alcoa with tax breaks/relief that, whilst making the project attractive to the company, minimised the economic benefit to the host country. For example, the government has said that company tax should not be counted on for the first fifteen years, suggesting that large tax breaks had already been promised to Alcoa. Local unions *the Greenland Employers Association* and the *Organisation of Greenlandic Employers* have warned that the only income from the project in its first few years will be tax paid by its employees, and with much of the workforce coming from abroad and on low wages this is likely to be very little.

Neither the Greenlandic- nor Icelandic Governments are going to admit publicly that they are offering cheap [electrical] energy to the likes of Alcoa.

---

[36] Aluminium Company of America

The Majorqaq is a meltwater river and valley having the same name, in the Qeqqata municipality in centre-west Greenland.

The Majorqaq is one of the widest rivers in western Greenland, draining the Greenland ice sheet. The river source at 65° 41'30" North, 50°32' west is an outflow glacier draining the Greenland ice sheet, in the far inland region of the country. The Majorqaq retains approximately the same width for the entire length of the river flow, from its source to its large delta carrying large quantities of glacial silt. The river flow is variable, with large patches of quick sands across its entire length, particularly near the delta. The river empties into Isortoq Fjord.

CNPC and CNOOC are the two [Chinese] companies that will likely make offers for exploration in western Greenland, in the area of the Disko Island and the Nuussuaq Peninsula, as Greenland seeks to increase its oil and gas revenues by opening up its onshore resources besides its offshore ones.

The island's deputy energy minister, Jorn Skov Nielsen, told Reuters "They have not been active in Greenland earlier. It's a new approach. We are moving the short-term strategy of licensing onshore."

According to a 2008 <u>estimate</u> by the U.S. Geological Survey, Greenland—the world's largest island—could contain as much as 17.53 billion barrels of crude as well as 148.21 trillion cu ft of natural gas. Including natural gas liquid resources, the total hydrocarbon estimate for the island was almost 52 billion barrels of oil equivalent. Yet, according to Irina Slav[37] China is not really the favourite candidate of Copenhagen: News agency Reuters recalls recent concern expressed by both the Danish and the U.S. governments over a proposal by Chinese companies to take part in financing and building airports in Greenland. Ultimately, Greenland quenched the concern by picking Denmark to help it to upgrade two local airports.

That apart, the autonomous Greenland government is naturally interested in pursuing business links with Chinese companies, which have the financial resources and the demand to potentially ensure a long-term market for Greenland oil and gas. According to Nielsen, Greenland's government planned to set up an office in Beijing in the near future.

The island itself, however, has a lot greener plans for its own energy needs: it currently sources 70 percent of its energy from hydropower and will aim to raise this to 100 percent by 2030.

---

[37] Irina Slav for Oilprice.com

Greenland had already planned to increase its share of renewable energy to 60% of total energy production by 2020. **It has a tremendous natural potential for renewable energy,** which among other things can be utilized for the development of emerging industry. Increasing focus in Greenland is being placed on small-scale solutions for renewable energy to be used in smaller towns and settlements where there is currently no access to hydopower. The Government of Greenland provides support for developing renewable energy projects, including micro hydropower plants, and solar and wind power that aim at a self-sufficient Greenland energy supply. Furthermore, the utilization of renewable energy in the transport sector is being explored. The development of renewable energy sources is a key issue in Greenland's international cooperation strategy.

ALUMINIUM SMELTING AT WHAT COST?

Any heavily subisidized electrical power deal with Alcoa will likely prove a serious burden to the national economy. Whilst for Greenland's Government, the smelting project symbolises an opportunity to come a step closer to economic independence from Denmark, **Iceland's experience has sent out some worrying signals.** It is therefore inevitable that both local- and central government in Greenland will attempt to sway public opinion by way of limiting the amount of sensitive information on the project that they are prepared to divulge. **The authorities in Maniitsoq** - where the aluminium smelter is planned - focus principally on the prospect of employment generation, rising incomes and increased economic wealth. Greenland's parliament, the **_Inatsisartut,_** was in no rush before taking the final vote on whether to give the 'go ahead' for the construction of this smelting plant, the first large industrial development in Greenland. They were playing their cards close to their chests, such was their desire to establish this smelting plant, even if the financial aspects had to be kept secret from the Greenland public and trades unions.

Given the many problems these caused in Iceland, there has therefore been a degree of caution in Greenland about taking on too much of the burden of construction costs and loans. To spread the financial risk, the Greenlandic government considered bringing a third party into co-ownership of the project instead of taking the whole of the 50% stake it was offered by Alcoa.

In the run up to Iceland's dramatic financial crash in 2008 the OECD concluded its country-specific report by warning Iceland that

'large scale public investments are inherently risky……. No major investments in energy-intensive projects, including those already in the planning phase, should proceed without prior evaluation within a transparent and comprehensive cost-benefit framework (including environmental impacts and inter-generational effects).'

Icelandic economist Thorsteinn Siglaugsson had already claimed that

"Kárahnjúkar will never make a profit, and the Icelandic taxpayer may well end up subsidising Alcoa".

A 2009 report by economist Indriði H. Þorláksson concluded that the [aluminium smelting] industry would reap negligible benefits for the Icelandic economy and possibly cause long term damage, and so should not be considered a way out of the financial crisis."

The final **political** decision on whether or not to give the go ahead for the first aluminium smelter in Greenland was taken before the summer 2012. Irrespective of the decision taken, it was claimed that the process used to reach it had created a more mature Greenland that had become 'a player' in the global economy rather than merely a target for decisions made by outsiders.

Concerns had been raised in Greenland's parliament that the island's economy was too fragile to accommodate major projects such as the Alcoa smelter venture, and that the island was rushing too hastily into metals (and oil field) developments before it had proper monitoring and legal systems in place to manage large-scale industrial schemes. The latest word [25/03/2020] is that the smelter proposal is `in hibernation.'

BASE-, RARE-EARTH AND OTHER PRECIOUS METALS

The island is an emerging source of **base- and precious metals** as well as gemstones, uranium, and **rare earth elements (REEs).** REEs have been nicknamed the `New Gold', such is the increasing global demand for them as key components for modern-day phone/computer technologies, wind-turbines, electric cars, etc. Key industries are daily finding new uses for REEs in very specialized shapes, and the future technology market will be dependent upon them. **China** is presently dominating global output as well as the supply of these **REEs,** which is particularly significant in the context of politically sensitive trade- barriers being erected by the US., Europe, Russia and China itself. **REEs include Scandium Oxide, Erbium Oxide, Neodymium Oxide and Ytterbium Oxide.**

A vast number of the properties of **REEs** are being investigated using modern processing, research and testing methods. This is in the context of a technological leap forward in various industries, notably smartphone technology, especially since usage is spreading rapidly across the globe.

So the global economic – and political - power game is being played out on Greenland's doorstep. Chinese investment clearly presents economic opportunities for Greenland, which has been seeking to diversify its economy away from a concentration on seafood, as well as significantly reducing its dependence upon the large annual **stipend/budgetary allowance given to the Greenland government by Denmark**. But there may well be considerable knock-on effects relating to a growing unease in Copenhagen and the United States. The US maintains an Air Force base at **Thule**, at the southern approach to Baffin Bay and the passage through from the North Atlantic to the Arctic Ocean. The US therefore closely monitor expanded Chinese economic activity on the island as well as being conscious of the eventual opening up of the north-west passage to global world shipping once the ice-cap has melted sufficiently.

The issue of mining in Greenland, and notably Chinese investment in that sector, has led to deliberations over what does and does not constitute a security issue, as well as whether Chinese economic interests in Greenland may play a rôle in ongoing debates over future Greenlandic independence. Another example of Denmark's "securitization" of Greenland's economic issues was the controversy and political outcry in 2018 over the possibility of Chinese investment in Greenland's airport expansion projects, which also prompted intervention from Copenhagen to waylay the Chinese bid.[38] In addition to the **Kvanefjeld** site, a Chinese firm is also part of a partnership with the Australian firm **Ironbark** for a zinc-mining project at **Citronen**

---

[38] January 2020: Concern over security-related issues pertaining to Chinese involvement in the construction of a new generation of nuclear power stations **in the UK** as well as the potential risks of involving the Chinese state-owned IT giant Huawei in the UK's high-tech security systems, echo Denmark's unease. Several governments around the world have blocked telecoms companies from using Huawei gear in next-generation 5G mobile networks, citing security concerns. **It is a well-known fact that the Peoples' Republic of China has invested heavily in infrastructure projects across the world**, including in Africa and Barbados, etc, thereby gaining a degree of influence in these places.

Fjord in Greenland's far north, and a Hong Kong company currently owns the mining rights for an iron deposit at **Isua**. In the area of fossil fuels, two Chinese energy firms, China National Petroleum Corp. (CNPC) and China National Offshore Oil Corp. (CNOOC) expressed interest in bidding for onshore oil and gas blocks opening up for surveys in western Greenland in 2021.

Fairly recently, Danish business experts have suggested that **the expanded rôle of Greenland in the playing-out of China's economic interests in the Arctic should prompt not only greater scrutiny from the governments of both Greenland and Denmark, but also discussions between the two governments about which types of foreign investment fall under what areas of the 2009 Self-Rule agreement.** Greenland finds itself as a key-player in the jostling of foreign mining interests, and the Chinese have wasted little time in positioning themselves at the forefront of what could be a revolution in extractive/processing industries on the island. The **Kvanefjeld** project may be the most visible example of China's economic presence in Greenland, though far from the only one. **The question is how might Chinese mining investment in Greenland spill over into the debates surrounding Greenland's political future.** One of the issues is the deployment of [?cheaper] Chinese labour at the expense of local employment.

Social issues also represent a major hurdle for politicians. **Greenland has one of the world's highest suicide rates**, especially among the indigenous **Inuit** population struggling to balance tensions between a traditional way of life and modernity.

According to a study by *the International Journal of Circumpolar Health*, suicide rates dramatically increased between 1960 and 1980 as **rapid infrastructure developments** - along with an influx of Danish workers - changed communities. Suicide rates in Greenland are seven times higher than in the U.S.

Any hope of independence is reliant upon tackling its economic-, social- and health issues. Retaining the revenues of the largest sectors in Greenland's economy – fishing and mining uranium – will be very important, but are only part of Greenland's complex survival strategy. It wants to break completely free of Denmark but cannot afford to sever the Danish handouts that it is heavily dependent upon. The Danish Government contributes about a half of the revenues of Greenland's Self-Rule government, which in turn employs more than 10,000 of the 25-26,000 currently employed in Greenland. The country is dependent upon the export of shrimps and fish but its limited earnings are far from sufficient to pay for infrastructural matters. Denmark is now only responsible for Greenland's foreign policy and its defence, but whilst Denmark is sufficiently wealthy to support Greenland in this respect, the onus lies with Greenland to make an initial approach; and their politicians' reluctance to do so stems from their desire to stand on their own two feet. But are Denmark's and Greenland's positions defensible, given the urgency of the situation in Greenland?

As the search for mineral resources (iron, uranium and rare-earth metals) intensifies, Greenland is facing an industrial and social revolution. Inward migration is set to explode, increasing pressure on a society barely able to accommodate its own population. Despite its growing economic importance in the group of circumpolar nations, **Greenland still finds itself torn between centuries of Inuit tradition and Western economic ambitions.**

CHAPTER FIVE:

GLOBAL WARMING

Global warming is now widely accepted as a rapidly establishing and over-arching destructive force that is gaining momentum, not only in respect of Greenland and its people, but the world as a whole. For those of us who accept that **the destruction of the protective ozone layer in the Earth's upper atmosphere** is increasing the exposure of planet Earth to abnormal heating from the sun's **ultra violet radiation** – and its consequences for climatic change - our planet has increasingly been at the receiving end of mistreatment by mankind. [39] Greenhouse gas

---

[39] The Earth's atmosphere comprises a sphere of gases some 500 km thick, with the lower [troposphere] layer containing most of the gases, with the next layer [stratosphere] containing the protective ozone gases. In sum, the atmospheric gases comprise **nitrogen** – about 78% - and **oxygen** – about 20%, along with water vapour and carbon dioxide. These latter 'trace' gases, notably CO2, absorb some of the sun's heat and are termed '**greenhouse gases**' because they warm the Earth sufficiently to make it an inhabitable planet. The CO2 is absorbed by the oceans, taken up by plants in the presence of sunlight [photosynthesis] and given off to the atmosphere during combustion. Thus active volcanoes and wild fires [see footnote 13 below], along with the respiration of plants and animals add to the CO2 content of the atmosphere. Methane, emitted by animals and marshes/bogs, along with water vapour, nitrous oxide, chloroflourocarbons [CFCs] – invented by Man to replace ammonia as a refrigerant - and ozone are other greenhouse gases. Cars, trucks, buses and electricity power stations consuming fossil fuels such as coal, gas and oil generate the **nitrous oxide** emissions. The CFCs both add to the greenhouse gases and to the destructive depletion of the STRATOSPHERIC OZONE, more so because they are long lasting and play a major part in greenhouse gas build up.

accumulation will result in an increase in average temperature level of the atmosphere. There will be two notable major effects of global warming: the initial heating results in the expansion of the oceans and a universal rise in sea levels, now exacerbated by the acceleration in glacier ice melt. Secondly, there will be an intensification of the hydrological cycle: more precipitation, cloudiness and evaporation. It was long-predicted that there will be changes in the distribution of rainfall and storms, with tropical climates expanding poleward to both north and south. Some scientists now acknowledge that we are at the point whereby we are not only seriously endangering our own lives – and those of future generations - but those of all the creatures and plants on our planet beyond the point of extinction of species. Yet in the turmoil of the power-struggles that preoccupy our nations' political leaders, **there is the voice of denial of global-warming. The denial of a world-changing phenomena resulting from the enhanced greenhouse effect** drowns out the cries of despair at the destruction caused by economic activities in both the developed- and undeveloped world that are steadily and irrationally breaking down the sophisticated ecological balance that once existed.[40][41] "In one hour", according to QI Elves, "the

---

[40] It is often politicians who refute the `irrefutable', likely because their job depends upon their `towing the line' of the vested interests who support them financially.

[41] 10.01.2020: Over the last few weeks, vast areas of southern and eastern Australia have experienced horrendous, unstoppable forest fires, which, merging together, have engulfed countless communities, resulting in significant fatalities and destroying countless homes and livelihoods of thousands of people, not to mention the enormous loss of wildlife, including kuala bears and huge swathes of vegetative cover. The country has been suffering very long periods of severe drought and soaring temperatures, meaning that because the forests and woodlands surrounding communities were parched, the native vegetation – including most notably the oil-rich eucalyptus trees -

Sun produces as much energy as the world's population uses in a year."

The Denial School may argue that what we are witnessing in Greenland, and across the world, in terms of the accelerated melting of glaciers, rising sea levels and climate-change is merely the reflection of an historical process of change that has been afoot for millions of years. After all, the Earth's crust sits on an unstable semi-viscous mantle-layer perpetually subject to movement brought about by the extraordinary heat and pressure exerted by the molten liquid within the Earth's core below. We witness tectonic plate movement and volcanic eruptions and other phenomena, all of which reflect the subduction or spreading/stretching of the Earth's mantle layer, along with the squashing and stretching of the tectonic plates and crust as they move around/across the Earth's globe. So are we trying to maintain a `STATUS QUO' that is impossible to achieve, or slow down inevitable changes?

Apart from its 'mountain-building' consequences, rupturing of the Earth's mantle will likely affect the temperature of the oceans. This subterranean activity results in the incremental

---

quickly and easily caught alight/exploded into flame as if supercharged tinder-boxes. The severe winds fanned the rapid fireballs indiscriminately, engulfing everything in their path. Thousands of voluntary firefighters have put their lives at risk in the fight to control the fires, though, in retrospect, the shortcomings of the network of firebreaks have been an issue. Residents from near Sydney suggest that the sheer distance between fire-breaks, combined with difficulty of access into these deep blocks of scrubby vegetation to control the fire spread have not helped and they are resigned to accepting that the occurrence of these fires is part of a much longer-term 'occurrence' of draughts and rains over which they have no control.

growth of lava build-up around 'lava hot-spot holes' in the punctured mantle on the ocean floor, with the lava outflowing

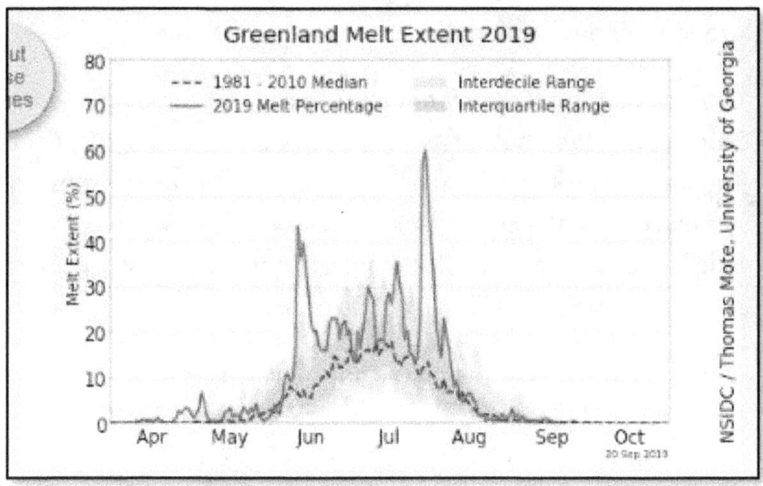

Greenland: Melt Extent, 2019; Source: NSIDC/Thomas Mote, University of Chicago

eventually rising about sea level to translate into volcanic peaks rising several thousand metres above sea level.

And these factors – when translated into air- and sea-currents - will in turn likely have a knock-on effect –albeit much longer-term - on climate- and weather-patterns, especially when operating alongside the reduction of the Earth's vegetative cover and its biodiversity due to short-sighted human behaviour and/or the forces of Nature, consequential or not. We only have to remember that **the Sahara Desert arose from manmade deforestation** many, many years ago, to acknowledge the fundamental impact of man's activities on climate change and vegetation zones. In a supposedly more informed world, are we likely to witness similar consequences as **the deforestation of the Amazon Rain Forest** currently proceeds apace? Or of accelerated ozone-layer destruction?[42]

Over supper on a sea-faring trip, we overhear a gentleman bemoaning the outbursts of a Swedish schoolgirl, Greta Thunberg, who has taken time off from her school-lessons and has plucked up the courage of her convictions to stand up to the louder voices of 'Global Commerce At Any Cost'. "She is scaremongering unnecessarily!" he blusters.

Therein lies the irony! For on the one hand we proudly pronounce how we are reducing our Carbon Footprint with Carbon Offsetting and bemoan the amount of plastic waste we are discarding across land and sea. Yet, as an increasingly consumerist society, we scrutinise every minute change in the cost of crude oil on the world's commodity markets and continue to churn out synthetic fabric clothing – based on the bi-products of oil refining - to replace the milliards of tonnes we throw away every year. Yet much of this discarded matter does not safely

---

[42] Brazil's loggers/lumbermen and farmers claim that –coffee plantations apart - clearance of the Rain Forest in order to grow soya beans is, on balance, a sounder economic proposition because the longer-term return from soya as a food-source, is greater than the retention of the forest. Naturally, this is refuted by ecologists, who remind us that it is the leaves of the living trees that - through photosynthesis - retain an enormous carbon bank and thereby counter man's damage of the ozone layer in the Earth's atmosphere. Yet is the mass planting of trees in temperate vegetation zones sufficient to offset the growing deforestation of the Amazon Rain Forest, the growing use of low-cost short haul air-flights and the relatively high cost of switching from petrol-engine cars to electric vehicles?

disintegrate over an acceptable period and can kill or seriously maim wildlife when dumped on land/ in landfill or in the oceans.

According to Leslie Hook of the UK's 'I' newspaper, the North Atlantic wind current is shifting course, with potentially huge implications for crops and sea-levels. For at the summit of Greenland's ice cap the temperature rarely rises above 0 degrees C, with only three instances recorded over the last 800 years, and when the ice cap surface melted in 2012 it was considered a 'freek' event. Yet according to Professor Konrad Steffen, between 30th July and 2nd August 2019, a heatwave in Greenland produced several record highs on the ice sheet, including the East Grip, the second highest monitoring station. Steffen's view is that "if you start melting at the top of the ice-sheet, we are going to lose [the] Greenland ice-sheet long term." Steffen put this melting down to a heatwave, the immediate trigger for which was a shift in atmospheric currents high above the earth's surface: the North Atlantic Jet Stream. This fast current of wind blows from west to east, the shift formed a buckle that was trapping warm air over Greenland, having caused a record-setting heatwave in Europe a few days earlier before travelling across Greenland. Tim Woollings of Oxford University believes that the Jet Stream is essentially the most important weather phenomenon for coming to grips with weather in the northern hemisphere. July 2019 was the joint hottest month ever recorded by modern instruments, and is attributed to the underlying warming of the planet, itself attributed to the burning of fossil fuels increasing level of CO2 in the atmosphere and the behaviour of the Jet Stream, resulting in some big heatwaves.

And according to journalist Dan McDougall, of the UK's *Guardian* newspaper[43], Greenland's ice melt has been adopted by the world as a '**bellwether for climate crisis**', **but the impact on biodiversity has been overlooked.** At an ice station on a remote Arctic glacier, scientists are looking to the smallest of life forms to predict the pace of species extinction. Glaciers might represent more than 10% of the Earth's landmass, and whilst they are breeding and spawning places for the familiar Arctic animal species, **are teeming with biodiversity, with the bacteria, fungi and algae having an increasing presence there.** They are spawning and breeding places not just for the familiar species like whales, arctic hares and foxes, polar bears, seals and muskoxen but also for bacteria, fungi and algae that have a vital role in determining the planet's biodiversity. According to microbiologists working on a glacier in South Eastern Greenland, algae represent a significant causal factor in the accelerating melting on glaciers, both in Greenland and elsewhere in the world. **Algae blooms, they say, are turning sun-reflecting glaciers into sun-absorbing hotspots.**

He also talks about how, in the end, the fate of our glaciers, sea-level rises and biodiversity loss, will not only come down to the excesses of the industrial age and our unbridled consumerism, but also to the influence of algae. The sticky green residue familiar from childhood tadpole ponds, as it turns out, could be a microscopic *bellwether* for this age of extinction.

Each year, high on Greenland's glaciers, algae perform a remarkable migration. After spending winter deep in the snowpack as dormant cysts, they awake in spring and swim through snowmelt, dividing and photosynthesizing along the route. When they reach the surface, the algae turn black, dark green and crimson – colours that come from astaxanthin, a

---

[43] "The Age of Extinction" last revised 07/11/2019

molecular cousin of the chemical that makes sweet potato orange.

The algae produce it as a sunscreen, as it absorbs UV light. Consequently, the humble algae dramatically reduce the amount of sunlight reflected by Greenland's glaciers and increase the sunlight they absorb, darkening the snow and ice. Most concerning is the fact the algae that live on the ice surface in summer are increasingly dark brown, leading them to absorb more sunlight and exacerbate melting.

Professor Liane Benning-Anesio and his colleague lead a team responsible for this breakthrough discovery. The team is now aiming to understand the mechanisms behind the algal growth, and how the organisms have adapted to live on the ice. The key question is whether the algae will grow and darken other areas of the ice sheet as the climate gets warmer. If this happens, which is what the team in **Sermilik** suspect, it will mean up to 30% faster melting of the ice sheet than existing models are predicting.

"In 2019 our glaciers and ice sheets [are] already being darkened by dust, soot, and ash from our industrial world, which provides the perfect home for algae to flourish," Anesio says. "As the organisms reproduce, they melt even more snow, which in turn allows them to proliferate again. So it's like a cycle. A very bad one." And as algae spread, the effect will be compounded, leading to even more melting.

Benning, of the German Research Centre for Geosciences or GFZ in Potsdam, was previously part of the Black and Bloom Project to understand how and why the Greenland ice sheet is melting. She says algae-discoloured snow isn't just an Arctic phenomenon. She says

"This is increasingly a problem in the Arctic, Alpine and Himalayan glaciers. Blooms of red snow and brown ice are turning up in Antarctica also... [by widening out our research, confirm that] this is a significant factor in ice melt. This is why we are back here in Greenland but we believe the work also needs to be done elsewhere."

Witnesses to the ice-melt compare it to a violent sonic boom, followed by an echoing machine-gun style reiteration as the iceberg turns on its axis, before surrendering to the ocean with an eerie silence.

On one single day last month, NASA's Oceans Melting Greenland project announced that Greenland's ice sheet had suffered its most substantial single-day volume loss on record, sending an estimated 12.5bn tonnes of ice pouring into the Arctic Ocean – a body of water that could cover the whole of England in five inches of water. If the Greenland ice sheet disappeared tomorrow, sea levels around the world would rise by seven metres and it is suggested that life, as we know it, would come to an end.

Glaciers are in universal retreat. By 2100 Alpine summits may have lost around nine-tenths of the ice that covered them in 2003. In western Canada, somewhere between 60% and 80% of the ice measured in 2005 will have disappeared and flowed into the sea, and the Bolivian glaciers will have lost almost half their mass in the last 50 years.

Sermilik's scientists argue for serious thinking and funding to understand glacier loss, and for Anesio,

"There is no question that the data we are seeing is concerning ….. One of the latest predictions is that there is a 10% chance for sea levels to rise by two metres in 2100. So maybe some people think 10% is not a great chance – but I don't think I would cross the street if I had a 10% chance [of being] hit by a truck.

"Our job as scientists is to create more accurate models and add to our global understanding of the climate crisis so that it can be used for politicians to take action – we hope, a little bit faster than is happening now."

As glaciers retreat from India to Greenland, biodiversity is being lost. According to the UN, one million species face extinction due to human influence. Such a collapse in biodiversity would wreak havoc on the interconnected ecosystems of the planet, putting humans at risk by compromising food sources, fouling clean water and air, and eroding defences against extreme weather such as hurricanes and floods.

Worryingly, as Greenland's ice melt has been adopted by the world as a **global *bellwether* for climate crisis**, less focus is being placed on the impact on biodiversity. This ice sheet is not just being melted by algae bloom and from above by warmer air temperatures. Arctic waters are reaching record high temperatures and warmer water is lapping against these great glaciers.

For Greenland, one of the least densely populated countries in the world, the impact will be felt on land by the nation's flowers, plants, bushes and heather, its polar bears, caribous, arctic hares, foxes and wolves and at sea by narwhals, seals, bowhead whales and the large variety of unique sea birds.

This is biodiversity that actually faces few direct pressures from human activities – the major threat is glacial melt and climate change. The shrinking of the sea ice area is already having a significant impact on marine ecosystems. It's an essential habitat and breeding ground for many species, ranging from micro-algae to marine mammals.

This is now a hungry time for polar bears struggling to access the sea ice to hunt for seals. An estimated 3,500 of the bears stalk the coastline of Greenland and at Sermilik, stories are swapped of close encounters with the animals.

Scientific labours in the chill winds and high seas of the Arctic summer seem wrapped in an unusual sense of urgency this year. The scientists working in Greenland are keen to communicate their new, emerging understanding of the dynamics of the declining ice sheet to the broader world.

According to **Christopher Trivedi**, a US member of the scientific team, communicating the work of the many scientists active across Greenland to local people is a vital and often overlooked part of the job. "I think science communication matters. We need to include the local community here with the work we are doing, and we also have a responsibility to explain the work we are doing here. What we are finding impacts the immediate environment more than anywhere else."

For the younger members of the Sermilik team, the bleakest conversation held at the ice station is around the plastic being discovered.

"We are finding plastics in the atmosphere at the centre of Greenland's ice sheet," says Dr James Bradley, assistant professor at the Queen Mary University of London. "Millions of tonnes of plastic are discarded into the environment every year and are broken down into small particles and fibres that do not biodegrade. These particles, known as microplastics, have now been found everywhere from high mountains to deep oceans and can carry toxic chemicals and harmful microbes. Their presence in oceans and waterways has received a great deal of scientific and media attention in recent years, but our growing concern is their presence in the atmosphere."

It is evident that all the scientists feel a growing responsibility on their shoulders to answer questions that have been ignored for too long. This summer, in the face of record ice melt, there is a deeper purpose and an urgency to their work. They want more resources and new technologies to map the details of ice loss with greater precision. They want better global monitoring of nutrients and contaminants that are now trickling at ever higher rates from glaciers into downstream waterways. They want to expand their work to Antarctica and other parts of the glacial world.

"To be honest, I'm massively worried," says Anesio. "I just hope that we are not crossing that tipping point because I don't think humans can adapt to the rates of changing climates at the moment."

He says that he also has hope, "because I can see a new movement in the young generation that cares. I think that everyone individually can contribute, by pressing politicians, but also by making their contribution in terms of the reduction of CO2."

Leaving the ice station by boat, negotiating the same narrow channel of icebergs that brought us here, we pass over the shattered remnants of a glacier and stop to scoop a 1,000-year-old chunk of ice from the water. These lumps of ice can only meet one path, drifting out into the Arctic sea at the mercy of winds and warm currents until they break apart into the ocean.

Days later, further north of the island, a local ship's captain summed things up with his Greenlandic dark humour. "That noise you hear out there. The fizzing and cracking," he tells me, cupping his ear to the wind for dramatic effect as his old wooden ship passes through a fjord filled with decaying mountains of ice.

"That noise is the end of the world."

CHAPTER SIX:

LIVING WITH CLIMATE CHANGE IN GREENLAND

Left on their own, the Greenlanders are relatively powerless to cope with the effects of climate change. The political- and economic 'bully-boys' in this ruthlessly competitive world have to be confronted by 'equal and opposite forces', to employ structural mechanics terminology!

The ice cap covering the majority of the island is melting at a quickening pace; and the melt-water is flooding down the island's rivers and its fjords and into both the Arctic Ocean and Northern Atlantic Ocean. This in turn is contributing to a steady rise in global sea levels that is already having a huge impact on communities living on the **littoral** of the world's oceans that cover 70% of the Earth's surface, forcing them to move to higher ground. According to a recent article in the UK's Financial Times and 'I' newspapers[44], about 200 cubic kilometres of ice disappeared from the surface of the Greenlandic ice-sheet in July, 2019 alone. That amount of water, if spread across an area the size of England – and contained at its edges! – would stand 1.5 metres deep. And the frozen arctic soil, called **permafrost**, contains more carbon than has ever been released by humans. As the Earth warms, permafrost thaws, releasing greenhouse gases into the atmosphere. These emissions, much like burning fossil fuels, contribute to global warming.

Permafrost changes will have a huge impact on the future climate, but **because** scientists do not know exactly how much carbon dioxide, methane, and nitrous oxide is likely to be released, permafrost emissions are often excluded from climate

---

[44] The article appeared in the 'I' newspaper on 24.09.2019

models. They recognise that the rapidly increasing level of carbon dioxide in the Earth's atmosphere is having a significant effect upon global warming and climate change, but they are not in unanimous agreement upon the impact of the **Jet Stream** – one of consequences of this warming - on weather-patterns, especially over Western Europe. The path and impact of the Jet Stream are issues taxing scientists across the world. The North Atlantic Jet Stream moves along some 7km above the earth's surface, with the temperature difference between the Equator and the cool Arctic creating a pressure difference and a narrow, powerful band of wind that is directed eastwards by the revolution of planet Earth.

Ilulissat, on the west coast of Greenland, saw highs of above 20 degrees Celsius during the heatwave of 2019, which is a new phenomenon for Greenland, with the persistent heat melting the **permafrost layer** under the soil, causing roads to buckle and house-foundations to shift, necessitating costly repairs. In the 1980s, engineers reassured builders about the permanence of the permafrost as a stable base to build upon. Now they view the `permafrost' change as a huge problem in that respect. Scientist Jennifer Francis[45] says

"We think that the rapidly warming Arctic is making these wavy patterns – in the Jet Stream – happen more often, and as a result we are seeing weather patterns themselves becoming much more persistent."

According to Professor Scaife of Exeter University and the UK Meteorological Office, climatic predictions suggest a pole-ward

---

[45] Senior Scientist at Woods Hole Research Centre in the United States

migration of the Jet Stream – albeit quite slowly – bringing milder and wetter weather to Northern Europe.

Most of Greenland is covered with permafrost – permanently frozen ground – ranging from 1.8m to 480m in depth. Structures therefore have to be elevated 90cm above the ground, using spreader footings, to avoid heat from the buildings melting the permafrost, rendering the ground unstable and causing the buildings to sink. The footings are laid some 3m below ground-level, with concrete columns rising up to support the floor system above the ground. Construction takes place during the summer and autumn, when the temperature is 10-14 degrees Celsius. Prefabrication of composite insulated components is important to the construction process, to speed on-site building erection. During winter, the construction work moves to the interior of the building, with the temperature outside falling perhaps to minus 17 degrees Celsius. The work inside will include mechanical-, electrical, plumbing and fire-protection systems. To take the town of Thule as an example, due to its proximity to the North Pole, the region has 24 hours' sunlight from May through to August, and 24 hours' darkness from November through to February.

This US military project, with elevated footings and `ground floor' framing, demonstrates allowance for under-floor ventilation and prevention of damage to the Permafrost layer below

CHAPTER SEVEN:

GREENLAND'S FUTURE DEVELOPMENT

Infrastructure development in the 1950s and 1960s did not expose Greenland to the full consequences of capital-generated development, nor have the growing mining activities of the 1990s and 2000s done so. In reality, it is not until now - with the aluminium smelter - that Greenland is really getting a taste of the capitalist economy with a huge multinational company like Alcoa as the major external player. Here discussions are primarily concerned with what such a multinational giant can do both for and to a small society like Greenland.

The fishing industry has effectively been industrialised since the 1960s, but due to the protected nature of the labour market, the full consequences were not fully appreciated. And for the construction industry, the *de facto* division of labour was said to be only an internal matter between Denmark and Greenland. Mining activities have attracted workers from across the global labour market but the consequences of this have not really been visible locally. It is not until quite recently with the planned construction of the aluminium smelter that Greenland really experienced being part of a global labour market. For some in Greenland, one of the major concerns was the prospect of having up to 3 000 Chinese workers constructing the aluminium smelter for 'international wages'.

NUUK: CITY OF OPPORTUNITY

Plans for the future include expansion of both port and airport. This is necessary, to ensure the supply lines can cope with continued development. With the growing interest in the Arctic, the 'Capital Strategy' reflects a desire for Nuuk to be the first choice when politicians, businesses and tourists look to the North, globally speaking. Nuuk's ambitious 'Capital Strategy' predicts that the city should have the capacity for 30,000 people by the year 2030[46]

GROWTH OF SISIMIUT

Over the last decade or more, **Sisimiut** has developed as a specialised industrial-, administrative- and educational-hub for the surrounding areas of Greenland. Its main source of income is shrimp fishing, with the world's largest shrimp-peeling factory located there. **Hunting is still an important local livelihood, with seals, walruses, belugas, narwhales, reindeers and muskoxen as the main targets**. A large housing-company, supply company and supermarket chain have their headquarters in the town. A significant number of students from Sisimiut itself and from other towns and settlements now attend the various schools and specialist colleges established in the town. The public debate about aluminium smelting, oil drilling etc. reflects a key change in the relationship between Greenland's Government and its people. Different groups of stakeholders have now become accustomed to questioning the information provided by the authorities for public consumption. Both national- and international environmentalists mistrust the results of official environmental studies, cultural protectionists are alarmed by the potential

---

[46] In an upbeat article in 'Greenland Today', in November, 2016

destruction of archaeological sites, labour organisations are concerned about the economic calculations provided by the

The ice core drilling project NEEM is the main topic in Kirsten Hvenegård-Lassen's paper on the story of Greenland. The story of a country with social problems is often allowed to shade the story of a country with enormous research potential, the lecturer says, and, critically, the Greenlanders are often kept out of the latter story. (Photo: NEEM ice core drilling project)

Government. Furthermore, advocates of greater democracy on the island point to the lack of democratic input into the political decision process. Of course, none of these issues is the sole preserve of Greenland, so in that sense, Greenland has taken its place on the world's political- and economic stages.

Yet, due to their financial muscle, Danish businessmen remain critical to the prosperity of Greenland's economy. **Natural resources were and are at the centre of debates about the country's future.**

Yet it was not until around 1900 that private entrepreneurs, scientists and administrators introduced the notion that the traditional/conservative/colonial approach to governance and the principal of isolating Greenland's pure and vulnerable hunting culture could be replaced by large-scale industrial ventures based on natural resources as part of the strategy for the island's long-term economic future. This transformation found favour with the 'colonial authorities', and modern-day sociologists argue that this new approach became the springboard for successive visions of a modern Greenland that emerged throughout the twentieth century right up to today.

In April, 2018, Greenland's 40,000 eligible voters delivered an indecisive verdict that led to coalition negotiations between rival parties in order to provide a working majority in Nuuk. **With only one international airport and no roads connecting the territory's 17 towns,** dog sleds were employed to carry ballots to polling stations across the vast island. A brittle economy and independence from Denmark were among the most pressing issues for Greenland's electorate. Greenland has been self-governing with its own parliament since 2009, 30 years after Denmark granted it autonomy. **Despite having abundant natural resources across its 811,000 mile squared land mass, Greenland relies on 3.6 billion Danish kroner ($591 million) of subsidies annually – some 60 percent of its annual budget.** Splitting from Denmark would relegate Greenland to the lowly status as one of the poorest European nations. So, whilst coalition talks were taking place at that time, Greenland's politicians knew they needed to tackle more problematic questions affecting the future of the sparsely populated Arctic 'nation'.

Ana Andrade, Greenland Analyst at the UK's *Economist* Intelligence Unit, recently commented that a close relationship between Denmark and Greenland could be fruitful for both regions.

"Independence has always been a recurring theme in politics in Greenland. Nevertheless, the central questions debated are not if independence should be pursued, but rather how fast and under what terms."

Ms. Andrade believes that boosting the economy through exploiting its natural resources could provide the platform it needs for independence. The speed of change in Greenland is another factor, and memories of the yearning of poorer East Germans for a return to **life before reunification** must resonate in Greenland as the leaders grapple with these issues.

Change is underway: Greenland is undergoing rapid transformation brought about by international politico-economic circumstances and corporate economics. In a changing, increasingly predatory world where the exploitation of economic assets holds sway, the Greenlandic people have been forced – almost 'overnight' - to become protective of its mineral wealth and to assert their own right to self-determination. The mining of uranium –likened to 'gold-rushing' - and speculation about the extent of its extraction were difficult issues, but there is an understandably collective resolve among the Greenlanders to retain the fruits of mineral exploitation for their own benefit. A growing political awareness amongst its small but expanding populace has led them to addressing their colonial relationship with Denmark and to a relatively new-found questioning of the presumption of subservience.

It is the emergence of China — a nation with no territorial claim to the Arctic — as a rising polar power that has the potential to shake up the competition for resources and influence in the Arctic region. As we have seen in relation to aluminium smelting plant construction and the exploitation of rare-earths, With its economic and naval power on the rise, China, with its growing economic- and naval power has begun underwriting Arctic development projects despite its lack of territory there, underscoring the region's growing global importance. As the ice continues to recede, a race is on to develop or buy into the projects that can best position states and companies to compete in the New Arctic. Now China is pushing its way into the Arctic, announcing recently its ambition to develop a 'Polar Silk Road' through the region as warming global temperatures open up new sea lanes and economic opportunities at the top of the world.

At a December meeting of climate scientists in New Orleans, a team from the US's National Oceanic and Atmospheric Administration declared that the Arctic as we've known it is now a thing of the past. Coining a new phrase — the New Arctic — they described the 'uptick' in ocean-surface warming_ and the decline in sea ice since 2000 as unprecedented in the past 1,500 years. The Arctic, they wrote, "shows no sign of returning to [the] reliably frozen region of past decades."

As the ice pulls back, giant corporations and governments are moving in. With $300 billion in projects at various stages of development, Russia is leading the super-powers' race for Arctic infrastructure development to capture the Arctic's vast oil- and natural gas reserves. The country has begun rejuvenating former Soviet-era naval facilities along its northern Arctic coastline to establish a series of seaports to take in the oil being drilled from its drilling-platforms on the Russian Continental Shelf offshore oilfield. Russia's ultimate goal to have between 20% and 30% of its oil production sourced in the Arctic by 2050.

On the scientific front, Danish journalist Kirsten Hvenegård-Lassen believes that the perception of **Greenland as a financial**

burden over-shadows the notion of Greenland as a politically-strategic asset yielding a significant financial return. As a consequence, says scientist Lassen, the Greenlandic population is excluded from the narratives of the scientific Greenland, and this is a problem:

"You have to remember that there are [actually] some people [living] in Greenland and you have to deal with that. Awareness of the relationship between Denmark and Greenland is on peoples' minds all the time in Greenland. So whilst It does not affect daily living in Denmark, in Greenland that relationship is completely impossible to ignore."

For Hvenegård-Lassen, Danish researchers who come to Greenland in the service of science could well remember to employ Greenlandic manpower in their projects. However, she believes that the onus is on Danish scientists to instigate this Greenlandic involvement.

"Consciousness of being in [a] territory belonging to others would be a big step, along with the Danes making a special effort to bring some Greenlanders along with them. Of course, it is also a matter of education, though there are [employment opportunities] where you do not need to be highly specialized."

According to **Dorthe Dahl-Jensen**[47], who was one of the researchers on the now completed NEEM ice-coring project[48],

---

[47] A professor at the Centre for Ice and Climate of Copenhagen's Niels Bohr Institute

[48] Between 2007 and 2011, a team of ice core researchers drilled through the ice sheet in North-West Greenland to retrieve ice from the previous interglacial, the Eemian, which ended about 115,000 years ago. Ice core samples from the Eemian will contribute to the

Danish researchers were very aware of the Greenlandic people when they worked in Greenland. She says that she and her colleagues always invited students and researchers from Greenland when they worked there. More recently, she has been working on the new EGRIP p, which had two Greenlandic doctors participating, though the availability of participating Greenlanders is an issue.

At the same time, Dorthe Dahl-Jensen[49] often collaborates with the Greenland Institute of Nature, Greenland's Center for Natural Research, and as a result of the many lectures she has given in Nuuk, the Danish scientist says she is becoming more recognized on the streets of Nuuk than in Copenhagen!

"For me, Greenlanders are completely my equals - and many number as my friends. The Greenlandic population is well educated and definitely the strongest Inuit population that everyone looks forward to. I think the colonial mind-set belongs to the previous generation. We need to move on," says Dorthe Dahl-Jensen.

Thus, the research collaboration between Danes and Greenlanders is already flourishing, says Dorthe Dahl-Jensen. This is also reflected in the fact that the University of Copenhagen has a permanent researcher in Nuuk, whose task, she says, is to promote research collaboration. The professor also feels that the Greenlandic people have a positive perception of the Danish researchers 'projects, which is seen in, among other things, Greenlandic media coverage of the researchers' work. The

---

understanding of the dynamics of climate under conditions similar to those of a future warming climate.

[49] a professor at the Centre for Ice and Climate at the University of Copenhagen's Niels Bohr Institute

relationship between Danes and Greenlanders in research is therefore blossoms, says Dorthe Dahl-Jensen.

Plate 2: A 1980s housing-scheme designed for a client in Greenland by the Danish architectural practice Friis & Moltke. Images of drawings and site-layout model courtesy of the architects

Plate 3: An early housing-scheme designed for a client in Greenland by the Danish architectural practice Friis & Moltke. Images of elevations, courtesy of the architects

of the public administration. The Home Rule government supported the establishment of cooperative ownership with up to 50% of the costs financed through special loans.

At the beginning of the new millennium, a new and financially stronger middle-income group began to dominate the housing market in a number of towns, and most visibly in the capital, Nuuk. Here for the first time a whole area was established with only privately owned houses and flats operating more or less on market-terms.

The process of developing a growing housing market operating, more or less, on market terms is expected to be replicated in the four new 'administrative' towns, one in each of the four municipalities created in 2009, and perhaps in a few other villages.

The establishment of Home Rule in 1979 signalled a shift towards architecture which linked old and new expressions. Big towns such as Sisimiut, Qaqortoq and the new Nuuk suburb, Nuussuaq, saw a return to the colourful wooden houses typical of the colonial period and spacious, light dwellings were erected standing two-three storeys high. A wide range of colours were used, and purple, pink and orange also appeared in the urban landscape.

As I write, forecasters cannot predict whether the housing bubble in Greenland will burst. If it does, it will impact a large group of middle-income citizens, but it will probably not really affect the exclusive little group of appropriately named 'housing matadors', who have benefited enormously from the housing boom aided by the Home Rule system. The availability of capital is always key and when an opportunity arises for businessmen to reap a good return, they can hardly be blamed! Nevertheless, poorer people still need better homes and must be the challenge of Greenland's Administration to ensure that the mistakes of the past are not whether Greenlandic, Danish or whatever – are employed to meet that challenge.

By way of comparison, it is striking to observe the current state of the housing market in, for example, the high north of Canada. In **Nunavut** and in **Nunavik** the housing market structure shows remarkable similarities to that of Greenland some 40 or 50 years ago. It will therefore be interesting to see how the housing market in these parts of the Arctic will develop in the future.

The international architectural elite has also been attracted to design some of Greenland's prominent buildings. The Danish architect **Dorthe Mandrup** has designed the proposed visitors' centre at **Ilulissat Icefjord**, and in **Nuuk** the Danish **Bjarke Ingels Group** has won the procurement to design the country's new national gallery.

Architecturally, the University of Greenland and the Greenland Institute of Natural Resources have broken away from the box-like structures whilst the use of natural materials enables the campus to blend into the surrounding landscape. **Belatedly, people in power are accepting that architecture/construction needs to respect and respond to the nature of the environment and the character of Greenland's people.**

The innovative new correctional facility in Nuuk is an excellent example of this trend. The facility was the subject of an international competition, with constructor **Ramboll** winning the assignment in 2013, alongside a design team consisting of **Schmidt Hammer Lassen** architects, **Friis & Moltke** architects and the landscape architects **Møller & Grønborg**. The design competition was organized by the Danish Ministry of Justice's probation service.

The new correctional facility will be opened in April 2020. Not only is it one of the most beautifully located facilities in the world, it will provide those sentenced with an opportunity to serve time closer to their families, nature and culture. The very idea underlying the project is to add qualities to the complex that will enhance rehabilitation and diminish physical and psychological violence. It aims simultaneously to provide a good working environment for the employees of the facility and a positive environment for the rehabilitation of the inmates. The residential units have been designed to bring the experience of natural elements such as changing day light, snow, ice, rocks, moss and blue sky into the complex. The wide windows in the common lounge area of each residential unit offers panoramic views of the vast natural surroundings. The inmates will also have an uninterrupted view of the expansive sea through the windows in their cells. The whole idea behind the project is to add qualities to the complex that will enhance rehabilitation and diminish physical and psychological violence.

This **Ny Anstalt Correctional Facility** will have a gross floor area of around 8,000m2 (86,111ft2) and comprise five residential blocks featuring 76 rooms in both open and closed sections. The palette of building materials for the project includes concrete, wood and weathering steel, which fit naturally into the vast landscape, helping to integrate with the open Greenlandic mountain landscape by way of its contrasting beauty and roughness.

Other facilities provided at the prison include employment and leisure facilities for the inmates, visitor spaces, office accommodation for administration staff and parking spaces. The building will also feature elaborate technical and security installations. The outdoor areas of the building complex include fencing and arrival roads.

Community buildings in **Taseralik, Sisimiut and Katuaq in Nuuk**, stand out as characteristically larger modern edifices. And Katuaq's architecture has been decorated by a number of the country's leading artists. Furthermore, many people regard Nuuk's swimming baths, called the Malik, as the most beautiful of their kind in the Nordic countries. The wave-shaped roof was inspired by the building's Greenlandic name: **Malik** means wave. From the pool, swimmers have a matchless view of the fjord and hills that open out beyond the enormous panoramic windows.

THE ROLE OF NEW TECHNOLOGIES IN GREENLAND[50]

Greenland today relies upon a variety of energy sources for electricity production and boat propulsion, although the Alcoa aluminium smelter project would see hydroelectric power taking on prime importance.

In Greenland – along with Jan Mayen and Svalbard[51] - a very large proportion of all space heating is based on fossil fuels. The difference in total cost between electrification and fossil fuels is

---

[50] Source: *'Energy in the west Nordics and the Arctic'*
[51] In Iceland, only a very small proportion (0.5%) of space heating remains based on fossil fuels

still so small that consumers may not feel it is worth the effort to convert, and even minor distortions from taxes could tip the scale in favour of fossil fuels.

In Greenland and Svalbard, wind speeds do not conform to the standard [narrow] wind speed range of conventional turbines for the purposes of generating electricity (typically, they are too low). However, recent innovations in wind turbine design may allow regions such as Greenland with low average wind speed and high variability to enjoy the benefits of wind power.[52]

There are concerns over security, efficiency-losses and technological novelty in relation to **hydrogen production**, storage and conversion compared to straightforward battery technologies. But hydrogen advantages include flexibility, energy storage capabilities, synergy with intermittent renewable energy sources like wind and solar power and the lack of any real alternatives for very energy-intensive non-stationary uses, like ocean-going fishing vessels, cargo vessels and aeroplanes. Hydrogen-fuelled ships are not expected to be available in the Arctic Region before 2025, by which time, hydrogen-fuelled ships are assumed to have moved beyond the pilot testing phase.

Even though Greenland – along with other Arctic countries - has a vast coastline and most of the population living by the sea, tidal and wave power are discounted at the present due to their low development status in areas other than the commercial sector.

The technologies needed for a transition to renewable energy exist, and their prices are expected to become competitive within a very short timeframe. The major barriers to a green transition are no longer the availability or price of relevant technologies. What is needed now is not further public funding of R&D, but

---

[52]

rather a political focus on removing taxes and regulation that distort the competition between technologies.

A GREENER GREENLAND

From an economic perspective, Greenland has the potential to make a quick and low-cost transition to a low emission society. The first and most pressing task is to electrify all heating, a task that should be economically feasible today.

Energy prices are heavily regulated in order to provide equal opportunities for all Greenlanders regardless of where they live. Whilst the effect is to distort the market, this could be corrected with [for example] State subsidies to support private investment. The average *per capita* income is generally low, which adds to the challenge of financing the necessary private investment to significantly progress electrification of heating. That said, there are very large differences between the optimal paths to low-emission for towns and [the smaller] settlements in Greenland. In **Nuuk**, the main challenge will be balancing increased electrification with the need for higher energy-use efficiency throughout, in order not to exceed the capacity of the existing hydropower plant. So [for example] there would need to be increased thermal insulation and optimal technology to reduce electricity consumption for any given level of thermal comfort. By way of contrast, in **Ilulissat**, there is not much need for energy efficiency, due to the very large excess capacity of the hydropower plant. Instead, heating needs to be converted to electric boilers at the earliest convenience.

In the small settlements in Greenland, exemplified by **Atammik**, the path to reduced (carbon) emissions is less straightforward. A hybrid system being tested in **Igaliku** forms one of the first steps in the electrification of heating – preferably using heat pumps – in a low-emission environment.

Plate 4: Competition-winning correctional facility designed by Danish architects Friis & Moltke in collaboration with Schmidt Hammer Architects. The building complex is now under construction in Nuuk,

CHAPTER EIGHT:

SELF-DETERMINATION

According to Dr Klaus Georg Hansen[53], the Danish peoples' mind set mistakenly continues to regard Greenland's status as that of a colony that ceased with the constitutional amendment in 1953. This was the year when Greenland technically **moved <u>outside the kingdom</u>** and ceased being a **county <u>within the Danish kingdom.</u>** However, Dr Hansen believes that there are many natives of Greenland itself who no longer see it that way because they maintain that Greenland is technically still a Danish colony.[54]

Hansen believes that pre-recognition by both the Danish people and their Government of the fact that **Greenland is to all intents and purposes a colony** is fundamental to Denmark and Greenland together moving forward towards the true independence of Greenland. Greenlanders tacitly acknowledge their current colonial status – as an unspoken truth – whilst

---

[53] a member of Greenland's Executive and a distinguished expert on Greenland, its history and its people. Klaus Georg Hansen's [doctoral] dissertation is published as the book *'From passive observer to active participant'*, where he explains, among other things, the discourses that characterize our perception of Greenland.

[54] Colonialism has been defined as the policy or practice of acquiring full- or partial political control over another country, populating it with settlers and exploiting it economically.

choosing instead to focus upon furthering their unique decolonisation process.

Hansen believes that the general Danish public and the Danish press/media need a rethink, to clarify **that Greenland is no longer the backward and primitive prisoner society that many in Denmark continue to perceive it as being.** He considers that there is a discrepancy between the Danish perception of Greenland as a **non-colonial but backward society,** and the Greenlanders' understanding of Greenland as **a continuing colony but simultaneously a modern society of both good and bad.**

Hansen believes that Denmark has both enjoyed and continues to reap an economic dividend from Greenland. Thus, by virtue of its foreign-policy ownership of Greenland, Denmark regards itself as an Arctic superpower which, **Importantly, continues to exercise considerable political control over Greenland.**[55] This is particularly noticeable when we look at power division in Greenland. Currently, Greenland only has control over parts of the **legislature** and parts of the **executive**, whilst **it does not yet have independent control over the judiciary.**

Because of the unique culture of the Greenlanders and Denmark's interests as overlord, history shows that **the Danish interpretation of the 'native' Greenlanders' sense of the law** has not always corresponded with the Greenlanders' own perception of it. The Danish [police] historian Frederik Strand concluded:

---

[55] Readers may wish to ponder on who has more to lose if Scotland extracted the right from the UK Government/Parliament to break free from the UK, having voted domestically to do so.

"...[the] missionary **Hans Egede** – whose statue proudly stands in the centre of their capital Nuuk – [once] described [Greenlanders] as cold and unaccepting of the Bible's gospel, and as a `natural people' who needed to be treated in a special way."

Egede was not only a Christian missionary when he arrived in Greenland. He was also the 'King' and representative of the Bergen (Merchant Trading) Company.

The Greenlanders of the time had their own religion-based legal system, but the [Danish] King had not allowed Hans Egede to interfere. The Danish and Greenlandic legal systems were thus allowed to coexist in parallel, even though the Greenlanders' religious **jurisprudence** ran counter to Hans Egede's desire to convert them to Christianity.[56] The **priests** therefore had a law-enforcement function in relation to the expatriate Danes and Norwegians, but had to content themselves primarily with his missionary work amongst the indigenous Greenlandic population.

In 1782, the statesman Ove Høegh-Guldberg established by 'edict' that Greenland's dual legal system should be respected and that **the culture of the Inuit should be taken into account**. According to the historian Strand, there were several reasons for Denmark's relaxed attitude toward this dual system:

---

[56] **Whilst** Hans Egede came in search of descendants of the Vikings in Greenland, he did not find them, so his mission changed to working alongside the Inuit peoples and describing their culture in his book *'Perlustration'*.

First, Denmark wanted the Royal Greenland Trading Company to compete with English and Dutch trading companies in the colonization of Greenland. It was therefore in the Danes' interests that the Greenlandic population was settled and that they continued to hunt and catch fish that the Danes could sell.

Secondly, Høegh-Guldberg also stood for taking care of the weakest groups in society. At the same time, the prevailing wave of Enlightenment was marked by the notion that Greenland's 'natural' [native] people had special original characteristics which had not been distorted by 'civilization'. Høegh-Guldberg went on to make further pronouncements in relation to inter-marriage between the Danes and Greenlanders.

After the Danes' new constitution of 1849, they created a number of institutions for the Greenlanders, which allowed them to deal with crime themselves until 1954. Currently, people convicted on the island have been imprisoned in Denmark, but with the forthcoming opening of the new penal facility on the island, things will change.

Today's social issues represent a major hurdle for politicians. Greenland has one of the world's highest suicide rates, especially among the indigenous Inuit population struggling to balance tensions between a traditional way of life and modernity. According to a fairly recent study[57], suicide rates increased dramatically between 1960 and 1980 as **rapid infrastructure developments** and an influx of Danish workers altered communities. Suicide rates in Greenland are seven times higher than in the U.S.

---

[57] by the *International Journal of Circumpolar Health*;

Any hope of independence is reliant upon Greenland tackling its economic-, social- and health issues. Retaining the revenues of the largest sectors in Greenland's economy – fish- and shrimp exporting and mining uranium – is very important, but can only form part of Greenland's complex survival strategy. Greenland is confronting a load of issues but finds itself in an unenviable position: on the one hand, it wants to break completely free of Denmark but cannot afford to sever the Danish 'handouts' which it is heavily depended upon. **The Danish Government contributes about half of the revenues of Greenland's Self-Rule government, which in turn employs more than 10,000 of the 25-26,000 currently employed in Greenland.** The country's limited earnings are far from sufficient for paying for infrastructural matters such as the safe disposal of sewage and waste. Denmark is now only responsible for Greenland's foreign policy and its defence, but whilst Denmark is sufficiently wealthy to support Greenland in this respect, the onus lies with Greenland to make an initial approach; and their politicians' reluctance to do so stems from their desire to stand on their own two feet. But are Denmark's and Greenland's positions defensible, given the urgency of the situation in Greenland?

 Although Greenland has passed through five different colonial eras since 1832, it is claimed that a very large part of the Danish understanding of the relationship between Denmark and Greenland remains today heavily rooted in the now obsolete cultural-evolutionist way of thinking founded in 1832. In a similar way it is claimed that this 'outdated' understanding rooted in Denmark's population is therefore also embedded in journalists' 'treatment of issues concerning Greenland. Most times, it is expressed as an implicit and underlying view. For example, it is an oft-heard response to this day that Denmark must 'help' Greenland with this, that or the other.

This implicit logic, perpetuating the notion of the Greenlandic culture and people as more or less primitive, is a serious obstacle to a constructive development in the relationship between Denmark and Greenland.

Historically, the colonial relationship between Greenland and Denmark has had a large number of facets, **not the least of which has been the situation whereby Inuit Greenlandic women engaged in relationships with both the Danish administrators and Danish settlers in the nineteenth century.** The Danish administration's view seems to have been that ethnic differences need to dictate whether or not mixed relationships should be accepted or condoned, and it has been suggested that this amounted to a form of racial prejudice. Evidently, it became acceptable if Danish settlers joined up with Inuit women, though the idea of Danish administrators linking up with Inuit women was frowned upon by the Danish Colonialist authorities.

Although it has been said on occasions that Denmark must now excuse its colonial rule in Greenland, this is probably not the focus of most of the Greenlandic politicians. On the other hand, there is a much more pragmatic hope that in Denmark very soon, an internal, sincere Danish desire to look at the relationship between Denmark and Greenland emerges in a fundamentally new way, based on a new discourse. The starting point for the continued development of that relationship between the two countries would be an acceptance by the Danish that Greenland is technically a Danish colony today.

Over the past 50 years, Greenland has fundamentally changed its view of the relationship between the two countries, but Greenlanders feel that in Denmark there has not been a reciprocal view, and that its absence is hampering continued mutual cooperation both now and in the future.

INDEX

[subject to slight variation in printing]